CITIZENS OF HEAVEN
HOW EVANGELICALS SHOULD RESPOND TO TRUMPISM

ART McFARLANE

CITIZENS OF HEAVEN:
How Evangelicals Should Respond to Trumpism

Copyright © 2023 by Art McFarlane

Published by Lucid Books in Houston, TX
www.LucidBooks.com

All rights reserved. No part of this publication may be reproduced, stored in a retrieval system, or transmitted in any form by any means, electronic, mechanical, photocopy, recording, or otherwise, without the prior permission of the publisher, except as provided for by USA copyright law.

Scripture quotations marked (KJV) are taken from the King James Version (KJV): King James Version, public domain.

Scripture quotations marked (NLT) are taken from the Holy Bible, New Living Translation, copyright ©1996, 2004, 2015 by Tyndale House Foundation. Used by permission of Tyndale House Publishers, Carol Stream, Illinois 60188. All rights reserved.

Scripture quotations marked (NIV) are taken from the Holy Bible, New International Version®, NIV®. Copyright ©1973, 1978, 1984, 2011 by Biblica, Inc.™ Used by permission of Zondervan. All rights reserved worldwide. www.zondervan.com The "NIV" and "New International Version" are trademarks registered in the United States Patent and Trademark Office by Biblica, Inc.™

Scripture quotations marked (NCV) are taken from the New Century Version. Copyright © 2005 by Thomas Nelson, Inc. Used by permission. All rights reserved.

Bible text from the New Century Version® is not to be reproduced in copies or otherwise by any means except as permitted in writing by Thomas Nelson Publishers, Attn: Bible Rights and Permissions, P.O. Box 141000, Nashville, TN 37214-1000.

ISBN: 978-1-63296-989-7
eISBN: 978-1-63296-632-2

Special Sales: Most Lucid Books titles are available in special quantity discounts. Custom imprinting or excerpting can also be done to fit special needs. Contact Lucid Books at Info@LucidBooks.com

An appeal to the white evangelical Church in America to rethink its views on nationalism and right-wing politics and begin practicing antiracism, Christ-centered political involvements and heavenly citizenship here on earth.

Contents

Introduction 1

Part 1
It's Time to Rethink Political Allegiances

Chapter 1: Biggest Con Job/Marketing Coup Ever? 9
Chapter 2: The Church Has Lost Its Way 23

Part 2
It's Time to Adopt an Antiracist Culture

Chapter 3: Is the Bible Racist? 51
Chapter 4: Is Donald Trump Racist? 61
Chapter 5: The Scourge of Racism in the Church 71
Chapter 6: White Supremacy in the Trump Era 89
Chapter 7: Key to Developing an Antiracist Culture 97
Chapter 8: So What Exactly is Racism? 117

Part 3
It's Time to Rethink White Nationalism
Chapter 9: Is America Specifically Ordained by God?....133
Chapter 10: How Should Christians Involve
Themselves in Politics?...153

Part 4
It's Time to Make Christ Lord of the Church
Chapter 11: The Church's Job: Agents
of Reconciliation..191
Chapter 12: The Church's Goal: Reflect
Heavenly Values...201

Notes 211
Acknowledgements...253

Introduction

The title of this book, *Citizens of Heaven: How Evangelicals Should Respond to Trumpism*, asserts that members of the white evangelical Church in America should rethink their allegiance to Donald Trump and his extremist take on Republican politics. I say extremist because Trump's views regarding matters like immigration, race, democratic governance and foreign policy are far removed from traditional Republican positions. (Traditional Republicans do not believe in issues like taking over the government if you lose an election or defunding the FBI.) My book title also asserts that the scriptural response to the Church's allegiances to Donald Trump and his views is to act like citizens of heaven. This means eschewing right-wing, might-makes-right political activism and replacing it with modeling Jesus to the degree that the world sees us—the Church—not as a political force but as citizens of heaven. And, most importantly, the world will begin saying, "I want what they have!"

Trump is no longer serving as president of the United

States. So why do his views matter? Because millions of Americans—including Christians—still cling to his philosophy of governance. It's become known as Trumpism: the racist, fascist, nationalistic ideology associated with keeping him—and people like him—in power.[1]

Political scientists and journalists are observing that for a number of reasons, Trumpism is here to stay. For starters, Trump gives recognition to and articulates the interest of the white working class as no other politician—of either party—has done before. As a result, the white working class 'base,' who hitherto felt ignored, now feels empowered like never before.[2] Many of these people are first-time voters who believe in the goals espoused by Trump.[3]

Second, Trump tapped into white racism, which often masquerades as concern for what the former president describes as liberal immigration policies on the part of Democrats. In fact, Trump's rant that Mexico is sending us "rapists and murderers," his statement that the US should clamp down on admitting immigrants from "shi***** countries" like Haiti and some African nations, and his 2017 executive order banning travel from some Muslim countries were received without a whimper of dissent from the white evangelical Church or other parts of the Trumpian base.

Third, Trump introduced a 'bull in a China shop' approach to American politics in which he ignores laws, policies and norms in order to advance his extremist agenda. He excoriated the other branches of government—Congress and the judiciary. He called for defunding the FBI. And, let's not forget, he led an insurrection against the US government. These actions on Trump's part resonate with much of the Republican base.

Fourth, Trump's 'America First' agenda also strikes a chord with much of the Republican base. Dating back to the World War I era, America First describes an approach to foreign policy in which the United States withdraws from international treaties and organizations. Trump's take on foreign policy is that as the most powerful country on the planet, the United States is so tough, so macho that we basically can call the shots internationally and go it alone. Trump's decision to withdraw from the Iran nuclear agreement, the Joint Comprehensive Plan of Action (JCPOA), is perhaps the most blatant example of Trump's America First initiative. The agreement calls for Iran to dismantle much of its nuclear program and open its facilities to international inspections in exchange for billions of dollars' worth of sanctions relief. (The Biden administration is working to reinstate the agreement.) Yet, the Republican party and Trump's base continue to rally behind the America First concept.

Several elected and would-be-elected leaders within the Republican party have begun to use the Trumpian playbook. For example, at this writing, Florida governor Ron DeSantis has implemented policies to remove any real or perceived negative references to white people from history and social studies textbooks in the state of Florida. North Dakota, Florida and other states have passed or are mulling laws that essentially prohibit transgender girls and women from joining female sports teams in K-12 and college.[4] In 2022, Republican Kari Lake lost the race for Arizona governor to Democrat Katie Hobbs. Yet, without evidence, Lake refused to concede, citing nonexistent problems with the ballots.[5]

An announcement of a virtual event sponsored by the Brennan Center for Justice sums up the state of Trumpism in America. The headline exclaims: "The Republican Party has undergone a huge shift–from the party of Lincoln to the party of Trump."[6]

Who am I to take on the herculean task of writing this book? Three reasons. First, I am a Christian who loves the Church and would like to see the 'body of Christ' in America become such of a powerhouse of godliness that people will be brought to faith in Christ like never before. I committed my life to Christ when I was nine years old and have been part of the Church ever since. I also received training in Bible, marketing and management.

I have been part of the evangelical Church in America since I immigrated from Jamaica decades ago. Over the years, I have served in several capacities, including as an elder, Sunday school teacher and youth leader. In addition, I was director of marketing for one of the largest Christian ministries in the USA. I have led or participated in mission trips to places like Jamaica and Malawi. What's more, in the 1980s, I served on the steering committee for a Leighton Ford Crusade, associated with the Billy Graham Evangelistic Association.

A few years ago, I stopped attending a white megachurch because the leaders failed to denounce the moral filth, corruption and degenerate positions of Donald Trump and his followers. I told the senior pastor, who I will call Pastor Greg, that he could call the nation to righteousness without mentioning Trump by name. The pastor replied, "But I like his fiscal policies." He also said that if he denounced Trump's conduct—directly or indirectly—members would leave the church in droves.

In the ensuing chapters, I address the dichotomy of the evangelical Church's emphasis on holy living while it accepts the ungodly practices espoused by Trumpism—practices that are alive and well today.

The second reason I wrote the book is because as a marketing professional, I have observed that Trump's words and actions leading up to his presidency and since, represent a textbook case of successful advertising and marketing. Stated differently, Trump is so adept at marketing and branding that he conned the Church to forsake its core beliefs to follow him. I will delve into this matter in chapter 1.

My third reason for writing this book is that as a person of color, I have been disappointed by the way in which the Church has missed the mark concerning treating fellow Christians of color as equals. I have done extensive research and writing on this subject. Beginning in chapter 3, I explain the role racism has played in the white Church in America from the birth of our country through the present day. I also present scriptural and practical ways in which the Church can become a dynamic antiracist body that reflects the international nature of the Church—a foretaste of heaven when people from all tribes, nations and tongues will gather to worship the King of Kings and Lord of Lords.

I'm preparing you for this book like my doctor got me ready for an appendectomy several years ago. First, tell the 'bad news.' My doctor told me that the pain I was feeling in the lower right side of my abdomen was due to an inflamed appendix. The pain may fluctuate in intensity. But it would never go away. If the appendix is not removed, it would release toxins which would show up in my blood stream. And if the appendix ruptures, it would spill toxins that would circulate throughout my body. I would become very sick, and I could die!

Then, the doctor presented the 'good news.' A surgeon would make a tiny incision in my lower right abdomen, remove the appendix, stitch the incisions, and voila! In a short time, I would return to my active lifestyle better than before. Because the appendix will never regrow!

So, as you read through the historical and present-day 'ouchies' I present, hang tight. Because it gets better. Here goes:

Part 1
It's Time to Rethink Political Allegiances

Don't team up with those who are unbelievers. How can righteousness be a partner with wickedness? How can light live with darkness?

2 Corinthians 6:14 (NLT)

Chapter 1
Biggest Con Job/ Marketing Coup Ever?

"You're so good at selling, you could sell ice to an Eskimo." That's a compliment or criticism, depending on who's doing the talking. Can you really sell a product, service or idea to someone who is diametrically opposed to it? If so, how do we explain tens of millions of American Christians supporting Donald Trump and his extremist viewpoints when Trump shows zero evidence of spirituality? After participating in a prayer meeting in which faith leaders laid hands on him, Trump turned to his then attorney and confidant Michael Cohen and said, "Can you believe people believe that bull****?" Also, Trump repeatedly mocked and ridiculed evangelicals behind their backs.[1]

Yet, white evangelicals voted for Trump in such large numbers during the 2016 election that he won the presidency. Trump's election victory represents what may be the greatest marketing coup of all time! As I saw the presidential campaign and election unfold in real time, it dawned on me that Trump's victory was due—in no small measure—to his mastery of sales techniques marketers like me use on a daily basis. Here are seven of these techniques:

1. Develop familiarity with your target audience

For a short time, I sold cars. While receiving sales training, the owner of the dealership advised, "To be successful, try to find something in common with your customer, and try to get your customer to like you."

Good advice. Marketers try to identify with their target audience as much as possible. For example, commercials promoting Lincoln luxury cars show actor Matthew McConaughey behind the steering wheel. He's super-cool, sophisticated, upscale and confident. The target audience sees themselves in McConaughey and responds positively to Lincoln.

Or, consider the Culver's fast food commercials which features the middle-age pitchman and Culver employees in a lush Wisconsin field as they present the rural spirit and great food of the dairy state—available at Culver restaurants, of course.

In the field of politics, each politician is his or her own brand. As such, politicians try to identify with their audience as much as possible. Take President Joe Biden. His personal net worth is estimated at $9 million. But you couldn't tell this from his speeches. To identify with his supporters, Biden routinely talks about his working-class beginnings in Scranton, Penna.

But Donald Trump took identification with his audience to a whole new level. The former one-term president touts that he is a billionaire who controls numerous business interests. Yet, in his speeches, rants and social media posts, he routinely plays the part of the underdog. People or government agencies who oppose him treat him 'unfairly.' And everyone is always after him. "They're coming after me, and they're coming after you, too," he likes to say.

Trump has a long history as a pro-choice advocate. In 1999, he told Tim Russert on *Meet the Press,* "I am very pro-choice ... I am strongly pro-choice ... I am pro-choice in every respect." He also said that if he became president, he would not ban partial-birth abortions.[2] But not surprisingly, in 2015, Trump switched to a pro-life stance when he decided to run for the presidency as a Republican. The reason? To convince evangelicals to vote for him.

The former reality TV star also voiced support for the nation of Israel and advocated that churches would be free to endorse political canidates.

Trump told reporters that he does not go to church very often. Yet, he attempted to quote scripture by saying "Two Corinthians ... ." That's something Christians *never* say. Of course, Christians refer to the Apostle Paul's second book of Corinthians as Second Corinthians.

In his book, *The Invisible Promise: A Field Guide to*

Marketing in an Upside-Down World, marketing guru and *New York Times* Bestselling Author Harry Beckwith observes, "Experts on marriage agree that it is not common interests or personalities that bind successful couples. It is strongly shared values. And it's true of all great relationships."[3]

Trump repeatedly touted Christian values, and the white evangelical Church bought it!

2. Move hearts—not intellects

A marketing professor I had in college gave the class some advice I will never forget: "Don't sell the bacon. Sell the sizzle." People don't buy products based on facts. They buy based on feelings—how the product looks, feels and smells. What the product does—or is perceived to do—for them.

Take the Mustang GT. On Ford's website, you have to dig deep to find out details about the engine and transmission. That's the 'bacon.' Instead, Ford leads off by describing how the car makes you *feel*.

> "*Here's Your Daily Dose of Dopamine.* From the roar of the engine to its unmistakable style, a Mustang® coupe or convertible will raise your heart rate and stir your soul. Drawing on deep performance roots, every model features precise handling, high-powered engines and iconic design."[4]

In the mid-1950s, Marlboro cigarettes owned about 1 percent of the cigarette market in the US. But ad agency Leo

Burnett changed that when the agency created the Marlboro Man ad campaign. The ads did not talk about stuff like the quality of the tobacco or the presence of filters. Rather, the ads showed a ruggedly handsome guy in Western gear and Western settings. And there was one constant: The Marlboro Man always had a cigarette—sans smoke—in his mouth or in his hand.

The Marlboro campaign did not sell Marlboro cigarettes as much as it sold the lifestyle of freedom, adventure and manliness. Men who smoked Marlboro were a bit better than those who didn't. Within four short years, Marlboro became the best-selling cigarette in the world.[5]

Speaking to this issue of reaching the heart, Beckwith points out that people respond to messaging that makes them feel something more than messages that 'educate' them. "We buy with our hearts. We buy time and again with our feelings,"[6] he says.

Trump succeeded in reaching the hearts of white evangelicals. He knew that evangelicals care a lot about abortion and the nation of Israel. So, he adopted a pro-life and pro-Israel stance.

He knew that evangelicals were leery about Muslims and illegal immigration. So, he advocated a clampdown on immigration for Muslim countries and called for a wall on our southern border.

He knew that white evangelicals feel that the 'liberal' media and society in general tend to present Christian ideals in a negative manner. So, he concocted an 'us versus them' agenda and claimed he would be the champions of Christians.

And the white evangelical Church opened its heart and invited Trump in!

3. Be unique and communicate a unique message

Consumers are an interesting bunch. On the one hand, we push back when asked to change. Yet, we embrace new things which make our lives easier. And we welcome new ideas that build on convictions we already hold dear.

This is why the word 'new' and even—gulp—the term 'new improved' are among the most popular terms in marketing communications. How many times have we seen phrases like "New Look," "New Formula," "New Size" or "Improved Taste" in commercials and print media—and on packaging!

In the words of Beckwith, "Marketing's job is to convey that uniqueness."[7] He also says, "The greater the competition, the more the need for distinction."[8]

Leading up to the 2016 presidential campaign, Trump employed a number of strategies that were not used before—or used to the extent the former reality show host employed. Although Mike Pence was on the ticket, Trump basically ran the campaign as if he was the only candidate. His name was everywhere—on his private jet, hats, banners, placards, etc. Referring to the challenges of the presidential office, he said, "I alone can fix it." He did not promise to work with Congress or allies. He alone would remedy the nation's ills.

Compare this with other campaigns in which both the presidential and vice-presidential contenders for office essentially campaigned together. Think Obama-Biden, Bush-Chaney and Clinton-Gore.

Also, Trump campaigned with a level of braggadocio, swagger and divisiveness that had never been seen before in American politics. He asked his followers to make a personal allegiance to him. (Hitler also did this.) He goaded his supporters to beat up demonstrators. He called for the assignation of his rival, Hillary Clinton.

And white evangelicals gobbled it all up. As Kirstin Kobes Du Mez observes, "Evangelical support for Trump was no aberration. For many white evangelicals, the values Trump embodied aligned with the militancy at the heart of their faith."[9]

4. Use a slogan that uniquely presents your key message to your target audience

A good slogan or tagline needs to be short, catchy and represent the essence of the brand—or person in the case of a politician. The meaning should resonate with all stakeholders and have special significance to members of the target group. This is why so many taglines have double entendres. Take Toyota's tag, 'Let's Go Places.' The obvious meaning is that your Toyota will take you from point A to point B.

And the more subtle meaning is that Toyota inspires you to live life to the fullest and experience a quality of life like never before—wherever your adventures take you.

Trump's tagline, 'Make America Great Again' is in this genre. The former president could have chosen an optimistic and positive nationalistic theme, such as the 'shining light on a hill' metaphor made famous by former president Ronald Reagan during his farewell address to the nation. But he didn't choose an uplifting theme.

Or, he could have chosen an optimistic slogan, such as President Obama's tag, "Yes we can." The tagline communicated the message that we as Americans can overcome any obstacle and unite to get big things done for the good of the entire country.

But Trump did not choose a unifying, let's-accomplish-big-things-together theme. Rather, he chose a tagline that motivated white Americans to celebrate their white supremacist urges and 'return' the nation to the 'glory days' of white supremacy. It doesn't take a genius to figure out Trump's veiled message: America was 'great' when white people were successful in freely exerting white supremacy in the public space—such as during the segregated era of the 1940s, 50s and 60s.

In this regard, Robert P. Jones in his book, *White Too Long*, says Trump "evoked powerful fears about the loss of white Christian dominance amid a rapidly changing environment." And Trump accomplished this through his tagline and rhetoric.[10]

I can hear detractors saying that the 'Make America Great Again' tagline does not overtly proclaim white supremacy. Different people simply interpret the tagline in different ways, objectors might say. As a copywriter who has created numerous taglines over the years and who as written for major corporations, let me point out that successful tags do not blatantly make their desired point. They do so by cleverly utilizing code which both the sponsor and the desired audience understand.

Nike's 'Just Do it' tag inspires us to take action—to get past our personal limits in sports and in life. The iconic 'L'Oreal: Because You're Worth It' tag affirms women's self-worth and encourages them to feel empowered (of course, by using L'Oreal's cosmetics).

And the 'Let's Make America Great Again' tag gives white people the affirmation that Trump is specifically focused on their interests. And white evangelicals bought into it!

5. Use a short, snappy name

These days, short names are in vogue—for companies and people. Consider store names like Target, Kohl's and Macy's. Or social media companies like Twitter (renamed X), Pinterest and Facebook. Then there are singers with short names like Beyonce and Prince.

So, it's not surprising that master marketer Donald Trump simplified his name during his 2016 campaign (and since) to simply TRUMP. It's even on his private plane. Come to think of it, Trump plastered his 5-letter name on many of his businesses around the world. He also puts his name on numerous products—from apparel to digital trading cards.

Trump did not win the 2016 election because he brandished his name everywhere. But it certainly didn't hurt. As Beckwith puts it, "Think like a singer. Choose an easily remembered name."[11]

6. Assure your target audience that you will deliver for them

The act of promoting one's self, such as for political office, is much like promoting a service. If I'm selling you a product—such as a modern, Amish-built, solid hardwood home office desk—I would describe the superior cabinetmaking by craftsmen who learned their skills from an early age—skills that were handed down from their ancestors in the old country. I would describe the cutting-edge features like drawers that close with a gentle push. Plus, a desktop height you can raise or lower with the touch of a button. So you can work while seated or standing. Also, I'd tell you about the ports where you can plug in your electronic devices. You're able to 'see' the desk, 'smell' the cherry wood and 'run your fingers' over the silky-smooth finish—all in your mind!

'Selling' yourself for political office is different. Because there's nothing tangible to see, touch or smell. All you can do is make assurances. And this is what organizations that provide services do. State Farm promises that they will be there for you, "Like a Good Neighbor." Discover Card assures you that their card will pay you back. While Better Homes and Gardens Real Estate simply assures, "Expect better."

No presidential candidate in modern times made promises and gave assurances on the campaign trail like Donald Trump did. Presidential candidates normally say words to the effect that they will work with the other party and Congress to do thus and so. Not Trump. He just shouted a litany of assurances before his screaming, MAGA-hat-wearing supporters. Here are five of the top assurances Trump made to the American people while he ran for president:

- Build a wall on the US/Mexican border, and Mexico would pay for it
- Repeal and replace Obamacare
- Implement a massive tax reform plan that would provide a tax cut for all Americans—especially the middle class
- Ban all Muslims from entering the United States
- Create 25 million new jobs plus a 3.5 percent growth rate over the next 10 years[12]

Beckwith's advice to people providing services is, "Don't sell us. Assure us."[13] And Trump did exactly that. However, not only did he fail to make good on the above assurances, but the *New York Times* states that he broke about half of 100 promises made to the American people.[14]

Yet, the white evangelical Church believed Trump's wild, unsubstantiated promises and placed him into office.

7. Demean your competition

Comparative advertising has proven to be an effective way to differentiate one brand from the leading competitor—or all other brands. While competitive advertising is optional for brands like cars, computers and household items, it is inevitable in the world of political campaigns—especially presidential campaigns. This is because the electorate is called upon to vote for the Republican or the Democratic candidate. (Yeah, yeah, sometimes there are third party candidates and people sometimes 'write in' their choices. But you get my point.)

The goal of comparative advertising—or comparative positioning by a political candidate—is to differentiate yourself from the competition. In the world of business and politics, effective comparative positioning is usually civil and entertaining.

Take the famous Mac v. PC viruses comparison ad that many marketing insiders claim is the best comparison ad of all time. A stuffy-looking man—with khaki pants, dress shirt, jacket and spectacles—announces, "I'm a PC." Then, the younger, cooler guy beside him—wearing jeans, sneakers, a t-shirt and a sweater—comments, "And I'm a Mac. The PC guy begins to sneeze and blames it on a virus that's going around. The PC guy warns the Mac guy to stay away from him, but the Mac guy begins to wipe the PC guy's nose—oblivious about the prospect of catching the bug. Then the PC guy announces that he is about to crash. And he falls backward.[15]

The message is clear. PCs get viruses, Macs do not. Plus, Macs are cooler than PCs. The ad is hilarious and effective. Yet, it is civil. Even if you are a PC lover, you can't keep the smile off your face.

Move 180 degrees from this commercial, and you'll land on the Trump-Clinton comparisons a la Trump. The Republican candidate did not use the traditional rhetoric in separating himself from his opponent. I'm referring to statements like, 'she has a wrong vision for the country.' Rather, Trump used the most raucous, crude and defamatory terms to describe the former Secretary of State. Trump accused Clinton of being weak, unbalanced, unstable, dangerous and a pathological liar. She is close to being unhinged. And to top is off, he repeated called her 'crooked Hillary.'[16] And most despicable, Trump and his minions led supporters in chants of "Lock her up," over her use of a private e-mail server while she worked at the State Department.

Of course, Trump did not provide any support for his defamatory words. And his base, including millions of evangelicals, loved it. The irony is that the evangelical Church has roughly the same number of men and women. Yet, the Church—including women—tends to be misogynistic.

Another irony of the Church's support of Trump is that the Church teaches that people should speak to and about each other in a kind manner. Pastors, Sunday school teachers and small group leaders routinely quote the words of the Apostle Paul: "Let your conversation be always full of grace, seasoned with salt, so that you may know how to answer everyone," (Colossians 4:6 NIV). But strangely, this text did not apply to Trump!

Donald Trump effectively sold himself to the evangelical Church as God's choice for president of the United States. Was that sales job tantamount to selling ice to an Eskimo? Judging from the present status of the Church, apparently so.

Chapter 2

The Church Has Lost Its Way

My wife and I have a good friend, I'll call Maggie. She's a devout Christian who faithfully attends a vibrant evangelical church. Maggie also actively participates in a midweek Bible study. She frequently makes references to her faith in conversations and quotes scripture verses to buttress her points. From all appearances, Maggie is as good a born-again, Spirit-filled Christian as they come. What's more, Maggie is well-educated and holds a professional job.

Recently we had a conversation, and the subject of Donald Trump came up. To my surprise, I began to see a different Maggie. She justified every awful word, deed and action Trump did or said. Trump's hateful speech was just Trump being Trump. His lies were all due to the crafty video editing by the manipulative people at CNN and MSNBC. (Fox News, by contrast, is always "truthful" and "objective"—her words.) Trump's bragging about assaulting women is just male banter. Plus, Bill Clinton was no saint, she continued. Trump's so-called racist talk is all due to my misunderstanding him. And, to top it all off, Trump did not incite the attack on the US Capitol on January 6, 2021. Most attendees were women and children, and there were no weapons anywhere. Everything about Trump is noble, patriotic and right for America. And everything about Joe Biden is bad!

For Maggie, mysteriously, God's admonitions that Christians reject sinful behavior in oneself and others apply to everyone in the universe except Trump and his GOP followers. For them, anything and everything goes.

Unfortunately, there are millions of white evangelical Christians in America just like Maggie. The white Church in America has lost its way and is probably at its lowest ebb ever, in terms of credibility and moral authority. I say this because the Church is currently in lockstep with former president Donald Trump, Trump's right-wing followers and the white supremacist, anti-immigrant, divisive, lying, sedition-bent Trumpian movement.

Speaking to this dilemma, Joel A. Bowman Sr., founder and senior pastor of Temple of Faith Baptist Church, Louisville, Ken., argues, "Today's white evangelicals stand to lose much through their transactional connection to Trump. One could argue that they've already sold any Christian witness they might have had for a conservative majority on the Supreme Court."

Bowman further claims that white evangelicalism's preoccupation with power (through supporting Trump and the Republican party) has resulted in three things from which it may never recover: the rejection of objective truth, the reception of conspiracy theories and rebellion against legitimate authority.[1]

The very existence of the American Church might depend on whether and how Christians relate to Trump. In this regard, Jeff Brumley, senior news writer for *Baptist News Global*, says, "Continuing evangelical support for a scandal-ridden president is undermining the conservative white Church and could even spell the death of Christianity in the United States . . ."[2]

In fact, Miguel De La Torre, professor of social ethics and Latinx studies at the Iliff School of Theology in Denver, Colo., claims that the widespread publication of reports about Trump's affair with porn actress Stormy Daniels was "the last nail" for young people and the white conservative Church.

"Evangelicals have lost all moral authority," De La Torre says. The professor adds, "This current generation wants nothing to do with the hypocrisy of Christianity. We are rapidly approaching a post-U.S. Christian age."[3]

Christianity Today reports that one in two Americans believe that evangelical leaders' support for Trump has damaged the Church's credibility. The magazine also reports that, "One in four say evangelical support for Trump reduced their desire to participate in religion. And among evangelicals,

33 percent say their leaders' support of Trump made personal witness to friends and family more difficult."[4]

Or, to borrow the metaphors Jesus used in Matthew 5, the Church is in no condition to serve as 'salt' and 'light' in society today.

In this regard, Andy Stanley, founder of the Atlanta-based North Point Ministries, describes how many churches in America radically adhered to the pro-Trump agenda—in direct opposition to the Gospel of Christ.

> "The church or church leader who publicly aligns with a political party has relinquished their ability to make disciples of half their own nation, much less all nations. Intentionally—or even unintentionally—aligning a local church with a party or candidate is an unsurmountable obstacle to making disciples of those in the other party. Doing so alienates half the population."[5]

Stanley describes how his credibility was tarnished among some Christians because he appeared on CNN to explain his decision to suspend in-person church services at the height of the COVID pandemic. A longtime church member told Stanley that he was disappointed in him for appearing on CNN. It turns out the man had not seen the interview. He does not watch the network.

As a result of Stanley's decision not to take a political stand on the 'pulpit,' he received some horrific hate tweets:

"You are a heretic! Repent, before it's too late. You are a cancer to the body of Christ."

"You are a false teacher. Telling people not to believe the Bible. The Lord has a nice warm place waiting for you on judgment day."

"Andy Stanley ought to be silent and finish his days in repentance and mourning."

"You have got to be with Satan."

What 'sin' did Stanley commit to elicit this wrath from so-called Christians? He refused to publicly side with Donald Trump and the Republicans![6]

Other white evangelical churches were less overtly pro-Trumpian. But the decision of so many Christians to crown a racist, narcissistic swindler like Trump as their messiah was equally ungodly.

I attended such a church.

Once each year, usually around the Fourth of July, the megachurch gathered on a hill beside the church campus for a united Sunday morning service. I say united service because every other Sunday morning, the church convenes three services—at different times—in the sanctuary.

So, decked out in shorts, T-shirt and a cap—and with a lawn chair on my back—I made my way to a comfortable spot on the hillside. Along the way, I passed hundreds of other worshippers. A few older men caught my attention.

I noticed that they were wearing red hats emblazoned with the words, "MAKE AMERICA GREAT AGAIN."

I was tempted to ask them why they chose to wear an overtly racist and divisive hat to a worship service. In my mind, a Biden hat would have been equally deplorable. We came to worship God—or so I thought. And as such, political garb of any kind sends the wrong message.

The MAGA hats were like the tip of the iceberg. Because I learned to my chagrin that the pro-Trumpian agenda ran deep within the congregation. It showed up when the church's 'youth pastor' preached in the Sunday morning services. (I watched the service online due to the pandemic.) The previous week, millions of people around the world had demonstrated for racial equality in America following the police killing of George Floyd, a black man, in Minnesota.

Referring to the demonstrations, the youth pastor said that some people may think that the Church should focus on racial justice. Others, he argued, may say the emphasis should be on issues like abortion.

In the Zoom 'small church' (adult Sunday school class) that followed, I expressed disapproval of the false equivalency the youth pastor presented. "Why do we need to focus on either antiracism *or* abortion?" I asked. "Why can't we focus on both?"

All hell broke loose. The class leader (I'll call him Tom) and many other people in the class attacked me for being "too focused on race." I mentioned that I had previously lost a job due to racial discrimination and was forced to relocate with my family.

One guy my age asserted that the discrimination I experienced was all in the past. "I don't see Jews demonstrating in the streets. We all know how they were treated in World War 2," he said.

I responded that my son—who has dreadlocks—was pulled over by a police officer and harassed while heading back to college some years earlier. His major in college? Theology and worship leadership. I also mentioned that my son-in-law is a man of color. "I pray for their safety every night," I told the class.

Also, I told the class that my son's mixed-race wife—my daughter-in-law—was called a nigger in a small nearby town a years earlier.

Class leader Tom accused me of being angry and unspiritual. "You need to get back into the Word of God," he snarled.

Not one person in the all-white class defended me! My wife, who was with me—literally and figuratively—gave me a hug and discreetly stayed out of the conversation. (Any opinion she presented would 'obviously' be biased in my favor.)

One class member sent me a supportive email a few days later.

My request for prayer and support from the Sunday school class is not without precedent. Class members routinely shared their fears and concerns, and requested prayer support for a myriad of issues. Usually, people asked for prayers for health-related matters. However, one woman expressed concern for the welfare of her dog. She received more support and empathy for the dog than I received for my son and son-in-law!

That afternoon, I decided to check my e-mail before running some errands. I noticed an email in my 'In' box from Tom, the Sunday school class leader. The message opened with a 'cut-and-paste' statement from Dr. James Dobson, founder of the Christian ministry, Focus on the Family. In the statement, Dobson says that, "Trump appears to be tender to things of the Spirit." Dobson noted that he was one of about 25 Christian leaders who were serving on a faith advisory committee for Trump.

I assumed that Tom sent this info to convince me that his hero, Donald Trump, was a born-again believer.

Dobson grew up affiliated with the Church of the Nazarene, a Christian denomination in the Holiness tradition, which puts a lot of attention on personal piety. Maybe that's the reason Dobson said he cannot say with certainty that Trump is a believer.

That said, Dobson presented a potential excuse of Trump's sinful lifestyle: He hinted that Trump was still living "in the flesh" and that Christians—old and new—will "struggle with the flesh until the day of their death."

Tom was in essence presenting Trump as the saint. Next, he presented me as the sinner. "I know you have . . . experienced prejudices from others," Tom said, "But when are you going to get over it? The past is the past, and it won't change . . . You need help. You spew bitterness, you emote anger."

I felt like someone plunged a dagger into my chest. I made myself vulnerable to the class when I voiced my fear of my precious son and son-in-law potentially being hurt by racist police officers. And this is tantamount to spewing bitterness and emoting anger?

Then it dawned on me. A key element of racism is that the feelings of people of color don't matter. We don't feel pain like white people. We don't have 'real' feelings. We don't have 'real' families.

So, I thought I would change the subject. Clear my mind. I noticed that the CNN tab was open on my computer. I clicked on it and couldn't believe what I saw. On the screen was a report of a white police officer who pumped seven bullets into Jacob Blake, an unarmed, 29-year-old Black man in Kenosha, Wis.

That could have been me, my son or son-in-law, I thought. This happened today! I couldn't hold back the tears.

Participation in the choir was a high point of attending the megachurch. Just before choir practice each Wednesday night, choir members would chit-chat with each other. On one particular night, I overheard a woman sharing with another choir member how much she enjoys watching former Arkansas governor Mike Huckabee on television. She said she liked the fact that Huckabee published a kids' book that, "recognized the great accomplishments of President Trump."

I couldn't believe my ears. So, I checked out Huckabee's pro-Trump books. I considered the content sheer brainwashing. I wondered how a Baptist minister could paint a dreadful sinner like Trump as a leader with "great accomplishments." I wonder if Huckabee has come out with a book that whitewashes Trump's failed coup on January 6, 2021, when his supporters stormed the Capitol, assaulted police officers, racked up millions of dollars in damage and caused the death of several people?

Given the combined incidents of racial insensitivity and white supremacy at the megachurch, and the fact that the pulpit was silent on the daily diet of racism, lies, name calling, bullying, references to sexual violence and other such bile coming from the White House, I convened a meeting with the senior pastor. I told him about my frustrations regarding the racial insensitivities I experienced at the church. Several issues in our hour-long conversation bothered me. But a few left me dumbfounded.

Pastor Greg (not his real name) asked me what I thought about the Black Lives Matter Movement. I replied that I supported the goals of the organization. He then told me that he could not support the Black Lives Matter movement because he had reservations about the moral choices of the founder.

"What about Trump's moral failures?" I flashed back.

Pastor Greg went silent.

Then, he changed the subject. He told me that he does not find the concept of white privilege "helpful." I found his answer to be the typical privileged, white person's response to issues that disadvantage people of color: Denial. I can argue ad infinitum that I do not find the term, 'forced labor' helpful. But my hypocrisy would become apparent by my choice to wear cheap clothing made in sweatshops in Asia and other places. Since I benefit from forced labor, I can deny its existence till the cows come home!

Then to top it all off, Pastor Greg posed a question that told me how clueless he was about the plight of people of color and the matter of black identity. "Help me understand something about you," pastor Greg asked sheepishly.

"When you first started attending this church, I was not sure if you were Black or white," he recalled. "With your light skin, why are you so concerned about Black-related matters?"

I was so surprised by the pastor's question, I could not come up with an appropriate response on the spot. Didn't the megachurch pastor realize that in the eyes of white America, every person of color—irrespective of the shade of brown—is equally Black? Yes, Pastor Greg, light-skinned Black Americans like Halle Berry and Vanessa Williams are still considered Black. And these folks are as prone to articulate for the cause of racial equality as people with really dark skin.

I left the megachurch and started attending another church—this one in a mid-sized city nearby. I assumed that since there were more people of color in that church, I would not hear politicized rhetoric from the pulpit. Was I wrong! The pastor of the 'praise and worship'-style church waxed political in the weeks leading up to the November 2020 presidential election.

"I will never vote for a candidate who supports abortion," he screamed. He said his preference is to support candidates for political office who "stand with" the nation of Israel and who back 'pro-life' judges to the Supreme Court.

The implication was clear. Vote for Trump—not Biden. I was dismayed by the pastor's simplistic logic. I am pro-life. But I believe being pro-life goes beyond being pro-birth and means being pro-all of life—from birth to death.

I believe it's hypocritical for pastors to ask me to support Trump because of his 'pro-life' stand. The fact is, Trump has a long history as a believer in pro-choice. In 1999, he announced his pro-abortion views in an interview with Tim Russert on *Meet the Press*.

But not surprisingly, in 2015, Trump switched to a pro-life stance when he decided to run for the presidency as a Republican. Trump switched to a pro-life position in order to convince evangelicals to vote for him.[7]

So, is Trump really 'pro-life' today? You can't be pro-life when you order that babies be ripped from their mothers and put into cages.[8]

You can't be pro-life when you refuse to call for sensible gun safety legislation that can save countless American lives each year without robbing people of their Second Amendment rights.

You can't be pro-life when you learn that COVID-19—potentially the worst pandemic in 100 years—is about to strike the USA, but you tell the American public it's like the flu and will magically disappear. In fact, Trump told journalist Bob Woodward that shortly after the COVID plague hit, he was told that COVID could potentially be worse than the Spanish Flu of 1918, which claimed 50 million lives worldwide. Trump said that he did not want to upset the American people, so he did not tell the American people the truth.[9]

The Trump administration's former coronavirus advisor, Deborah Birks, M.D., estimated that up to 40 percent of the 738,000 COVID-19 deaths in the U.S. (in late 2021) could have been prevented had the Trump administration taken the necessary steps to curb the spread of the virus. Trump's lies and failure to warn the country about the dangers of COVID led directly to the death of close to 300,000 Americans.[10]

Let that sink in!

Given this overwhelming body of evidence, how can evangelicals claim that Trump is 'pro-life?'

I have been part of an evangelical Church for as long as I can remember. Indeed, from my childhood, I realized that the churches I attended attempted to use one standard for faith and conduct: The Bible. In fact, this adherence to the Bible, combined with a fair measure of youthful cynicism— led me, my siblings and friends to routinely recite a phrase when someone does or says something questionable: "Book, chapter and verse," we would say.

The message was clear. If a thought, action, idea or position/point of view runs contrary with Holy Scripture, you should repudiate it. As trite as the 'book, chapter and verse' mantra may sound, it helped clarify lots of issues for me over the years.

For example, if someone used the name of God while swearing, we would challenge them. Book, chapter and verse? The words of Exodus 20:7 would be recited, "Thou shalt not take the name of the LORD thy God in vain; for the LORD will not hold him guiltless that taketh his name in vain." (We only used the King James version of the Bible back then.)

On the other hand, the 'book, chapter and verse' mantra sometimes liberated us. For example, I remember being challenged by older people in our church who objected to trends like afros, bell-bottom pants and trendy music styles. I remember challenging my 'elders' to show me in the Bible where such trends were unscriptural. After some hemming and hawing, the older folks were unable to point to a specific scripture or scriptural principle.

So, we gleefully participated in the new trends. Over the years, I discovered that most Christians I met in person or through books and the mass media used some version of the 'book, chapter, verse' model.

That is, until Donald Trump conned the white Church in America. It appears to me, and to many other concerned Christians, that the Church bought into a 'pro-life,' pro-Israel, pro-small government, pro-stacking the Supreme Court with conservative justices to the degree that nothing else mattered position.

The evangelical's diabolical 'messiah'

Having grown up in the Church, I received teaching in the form of sermons, Sunday school class and youth group discussions, small group talks and the like from as far back as I can remember. The lessons called on me to live a holy, spotless life. With this in mind, I examined Trump's words and actions in the light of Scripture. Here is what I found:

Trump's immorality is a bridge too far. Many past presidents have had dalliances. But as president, Trump's sexual escapades place him in a league of his own. It's no secret that Trump has been accused of rape, sexual assault and sexual harassment by at least 26 women since the 1980s.[11] In the *Access Hollywood* tape, Trump bragged about sexually assaulting women.[12] Also, he paid $130,000 in hush money to adult film star Stormy Daniels.[13] Also, in 2023, a jury in New York found Trump guilty of sexually abusing advice columnist E. Jean Carroll in 1996. The jury awarded Carroll $5 million.[14]

Every church I have attended since childhood reprimanded or excommunicated anyone accused of sexual misconduct. Also, I cannot count the number of times church leaders—from Sunday school teachers to visiting evangelists—advocated sexual purity. They quoted Bible verses including, "You shall not commit adultery" (Exodus 20:14 - NIV). And they emphasize that 'adultery' in this context also includes sexual relationships involving unmarried people (fornication). Furthermore, preachers frequently recalled the words of Jesus in Matthew 5:28, which says, "Anyone who looks at a woman lustfully has already committed adultery with her in his heart."

Despite this, evangelicals accepted Trump with open arms. I guess rape, adultery and other sexual sins do not apply to Trump!

Evangelicals support a man who lies 32 times a day. Trump has lied more than any other public figure in US history. This by itself should have been the tipping point for evangelicals. Written during his one-term presidency, a *Washington Post* headline screams, "President Trump has made 15,413 false or misleading claims over 1,055 days."[15] From lying about the crowd size at his inauguration, Trump has made lying his daily habit. *The Independent* reports that Trump made about 32 false claims a day![16]

Like millions of other evangelicals, I was taught in Sunday school, "Lying lips are abomination to the Lord: but they that deal truly are his delight," (Proverbs 12:22 - KJV). So, it boggles my mind how evangelicals can bow at the feet of man who, in a paraphrased version of the old lawyer joke, lies every time his lips are moving.

Trump's record of stealing should give evangelicals pause. Trump refused to pay contractors or individual workers for services rendered. By withholding payment, Trump forced some of his creditors into bankruptcy. Trump's ploy was to tie up his creditors in court, drain their resources or force them to accept less money—or just give up.[17]

Also, a New York judge ordered Trump to pay $2 million

in damages to settle claims that the Trump Foundation misused (stole) funds.[18] In addition, Trump shelled out $25 million to settle a claim brought by former students at the now-defunct Trump University. The students claimed that the 'university' used false advertising and high-pressure sales techniques to arm-twist them into shelling out their money.[19] Yet, Trump's biggest heist was when he stole hundreds of classified documents from the White House and kept them in the unsecured, very public setting of his private home/resort in Florida. Trump said the documents are "Mine!"[20]

Every evangelical knows that the Bible says, "Thou shalt not steal," (Exodus 20:15 - KJV). And evangelical leaders would reprimand or excommunicate a church member for the kind of theft Trump has done. But, once again, evangelicals give Trump a pass for his dishonesty. Because, after all, he's their messiah!

As Kristin Kobes Du Mez claims in her book, *Jesus and John Wayne*, "By the time Trump arrived proclaiming himself their (the white Church's) savior, conservative white evangelicals had already traded a faith that privileges humanity and elevates 'the least of these' for one that derides gentleness as the province of wusses."[21]

Trump is no longer in power. But he has passed on the mantel of lies to his faithful supporters in the Republican party who are repeating the falsehood that the 2020 election was flawed. The irony is that many of the GOP members were voted into office on the same ballots they deemed fraudulent. This begs the question: If the flawed ballots put

Biden instead of Trump into office—and therefore must be discounted—shouldn't the GOP members discard those ballots for themselves, too?

Trump's mean-spiritedness seems to be okay with evangelicals. Donald Trump publicly mocked a reporter with a disability.[22] He instructed his security people to beat up protesters at his rallies. In at least one rally, Trump hinted that someone should assassinate Hillary Clinton.[23] And he floated the idea that police officers should rough up suspects when they're entering squad cars.[24]

Then there's the endless name-calling. Politicians traditionally voice their disapproval with the positions a political rival holds, while treating the rival with respect. For example, the late Senator John McCain took the mic from a supporter who was denouncing Barack Obama. McCain told the audience that Obama "is a decent family man—a citizen—that I just happen to have some disagreements with on fundamental issues. And this is what this campaign is all about."[25]

Not so with Trump. Once you cross him, watch out! He lambastes his critics in the vilest manner. In this regard, a long string of people have met his ire. From former Attorney General Jeff Sessions (whom he described as "dumb Southerner" and "mentally retarded")[26] to former President Barack Obama (whom he characterized as being Muslim.)[27] From former ambassador Marie Yovanovitch (who was fired after testifying against Trump in the ex-president's first impeachment)[28] to Swedish teenage climate activist Greta Thunberg (who Trump castigated as having "anger management" issues).[29]

Evangelicals routinely teach that Christians should conduct themselves in a "Christ-like manner" when faced with interpersonal conflicts. They routinely quote Romans 12:18, which says, "As far as it depends on you, live at peace with everyone." Evangelicals also cite the scripture, "Let your speech be always with grace, seasoned with salt," (Colossians 4:6 –KJV). Yet, these same evangelicals are so bent on 'letting Trump be Trump,' that they gladly jettison the Word of God regarding Trump's vindictive speech.

In fact, while delivering a speech at Liberty University, Trump joked about divorce and pre-nuptial agreements. He also urged students to 'get even' with people who wronged them in business. That comment triggered pushback in the media. However, Liberty's then chancellor and president Jerry Falwell, Jr. assured critics that Trump's statement represented the tough side of Christian doctrine and the ministry of Christ. Also, Trump's then fixer turned anti-Trump campaigner Michael Cohen cobbled a rebuttal asserting that Jesus 'got even' with his enemies by rising from the dead.[30]

As I look at the totality of Scripture, I am forced to conclude that one cannot claim Jesus Christ as Lord while paying allegiance to Trump. But, for reasons that defy logic, millions of evangelical Christians consider Trump to be their messiah.

Many people argue that supporting a political candidate does not mean endorsing everything the candidate did before he or she entered the race—or everything the candidate does in office. This argument makes sense.

However, there is no debate that supporting a candidate for political office is tantamount to enabling him or her to continue being the person he or she was before being elected. Indeed, pundits often refer to a politician's shortcomings as issues that are 'baked into' the politician's platform.

Stated differently, supporting a political candidate—especially a presidential candidate—means endorsing their positions on issues. Would evangelicals have supported an Islamic candidate? How about a candidate who stands for limiting Second Amendment rights? Or a candidate who favors keeping prayer out of schools?

The answer is no, no and no! So, by supporting Trump, evangelicals are saying that they are okay with anti-immigrant, white supremacy, hate speech and Islamophobia—among other hideous traits. It's that simple. And that scary!

Part of the reason the evangelical Church has been so eager to embrace the harsh, mean-spirited and downright ungodly actions and attitudes of Trumpers and many people on the right wing is that the Church has moved from its belief that public policy should reflect the teachings of Jesus. Numerous times over the years, I have heard and read preachers and writers say that the Founding Fathers 'founded' the nation on Christian principles. In one way or another, many of our presidents have referenced our goodness and decency as the elements that have made America great.

But Jerry Falwell, Jr., former president and chancellor of Liberty University, has a different view. Located in Lynchburg, Virginia, Liberty University is the world's largest

Christian university with more than 110,000 online and residential students.[31] This means the person at the helm of the university wields a great deal of influence.

In an interview with the *Washington Post*, reporter Joe Hiem asked Falwell, "You said recently that conservatives and Christians should stop electing nice guys. Aren't Christians supposed to be nice guys?"

Falwell responded, "It's . . . a distortion of the teachings of Jesus to say that what he taught us to do personally—to love our neighbors as ourselves, help the poor—can somehow be imputed on a nation." He continued, "It's a distortion of the teaching of Christ to say Jesus taught love and forgiveness and therefore the United States as a nation should be loving and forgiving...You almost have to believe that this is a theocracy to think that way, to think that public policy should be dictated by the teachings of Jesus."[32]

These words should send chills down the spine of everyone who considers himself or herself a Christian. The fact is that lots of our laws and public policy *have* been influenced by the teachings of Christ. In fact, the Republican party's pro-life agenda is fueled in large part on the teachings of the Bible.

What's more, if the teachings of Christ—including those about the sanctity of life and care for the poor and vulnerable—are not part of our public policy, there's nothing to stop the government from carrying out the most despicable actions. Indeed, the brutal regimes of tyrants and despots throughout history have all materialized in the absence of moral guardrails, such as those taught by Christ!

One of the most disturbing aspects of the white evangelical Church's fall from grace is the degree to which prominent evangelical leaders own up to, or even brag about, their allegiance to Trump and his minions.

Franklin Graham, son of the late evangelist Billy Graham is a notable example. He currently serves as president and CEO of the Billy Graham Evangelistic Association and of Samaritan's Purse, an international Christian relief organization. Graham believes God was instrumental in Trump's election as president. In November 2016, he told *The Washington Post*, "I believe that at this election, God showed up."[33]

Graham told the Associated Press that Trump's affair with Stormy Daniels is "nobody's business." Because for Graham and millions of other evangelicals, Trump is "God's anointed." Graham never once publicly denounced the lies, racism or accusations of sexual abuse, fraud and corruption that Trump did or was accused of doing. Rather, he defended Trump repeatedly.[34] In fact, the evangelist strongly opposed Trump's first impeachment, calling it an "unjust inquisition."[35]

An article in the *Atlantic* magazine cites a November 21 interview Graham had with Salem Radio Network talk-show host Eric Metaxas. In the interview, Graham suggested that "a demonic power" is behind people's attempts to undermine Trump.[36]

In December, 2019, *Christianity Today* (founded by Billy Graham) published an editorial calling for Trump's removal from office. Of course, Franklin Graham had to respond. He said, "For *Christianity Today* to side with the Democrat (sic) Party in a totally partisan attack on the President of the United States is unfathomable."[37]

Okay. So, bizarre as it sounds, Franklin Graham apparently accepted Trump as "God's chosen vessel" up until the morning of January 6, 2021. On that day, Trump incited thousands of his diehard supporters to storm the U.S. Capitol in order to stop Congress from certifying the election of Joe Biden as the new president of the United States. You would think that Graham would now distance himself from Trump. Think again! In response to Trump's insurrection attempt, the US Congress convened impeachment proceedings against the former president. Graham again voiced support for the man who fomented an insurrection against the United States. In a *Facebook* post, Graham compared the 10 Republican members of the House of Representatives who voted to impeach Trump to Judas Iscariot, suggesting that the Democrats had promised them "thirty pieces of silver."[38]

Let this settle in. Donald Trump orchestrated a coup d'état on the duly elected government of the United States of America. Hundreds of the participants have already been charged and are serving time in prison. Some of the leaders have been charged with sedition against the US government. Yet, for Franklin Graham, Trump is still "God's anointed."

In a January 1, 2019, article in the *Washington Post*, writer Joe Heim asked Jerry Falwell Jr. if there is anything Trump could do that would endanger his support.

Falwell answered in one word: "No."

Heim pressed: "That's the shortest answer we've had so far."

Falwell answered, "Only because I know that he (Trump) only wants what's best for this country . . . I can't imagine him doing anything that's not good for the country."[39]

If we take Falwell at his word, Trump's thousands of lies and threat, his division of the country along racial lines, his crude attacks on political rivals, his hostility toward immigrants of color, his attempts to bribe foreign officials and his refusal to tell the American people about the COVID-19 plague when he first heard about it in February, 2019 (which would have saved hundreds of thousands of lives)—are all for the "good of the country." I wonder if Falwell also thinks that Trump's attempts to overthrow the US government and install himself as an autocratic ruler is also for the "good of the country"?

I've often heard preachers warn about the dangers of acquiescence to ungodly patterns by referring to a frog in a slowly boiling pot. As a member of the reptile/amphibian family, a frog adjusts its body temperature to that of the ambient temperature. So, as the story goes, if you drop a frog in hot water, it will immediately jump out. However, if you place a frog in room-temperature water and slowly increase the temperature, its body will slowly adjust to the water temperature. Unlike a mammal or a bird that would jump out once the water gets uncomfortable, the frog would continue adjusting to the increasingly hot temperature until it reaches the point of no return.

This may well be a metaphor for the white Church in America. The Church has slowly accepted the sins of its political leaders to the point that moral authority and the teaching of Scripture cease to matter.

In 2 Corinthians 6:14 (NLT), the apostle Paul warned the church at Corinth, "Don't team up with those who are unbelievers. How can righteousness be a partner with wickedness? How can light live with darkness?"

May the Church move from the darkness of Trumpism into the light of Jesus and Jesus only. Another area in which the white Church in America needs to repent and change is in the area of race.

Part 2

It's Time to Adopt an Antiracist Culture

Peter began to speak: "I really understand now that to God every person is the same. In every country God accepts anyone who worships him and does what is right."

Acts 10:34–35 (NCV)

Chapter 3
Is the Bible Racist?

A number of factors in recent years have brought the issue of racism to the forefront of American life—and by extension to the evangelical Church. Consider the increased visibility being given to the police killings of unarmed African Americans, verdicts of high-profile cases like those of George Floyd and Ahmaud Arbery, Black Lives Matter protests, athletes 'taking the knee' at sports events and, of course, the racist rhetoric of right-wing leaders like Donald Trump.

This raises several questions: Is the Bible racist? Is Trump racist? Is the white Church racist? And what can be done from a Christian perspective to move from racism to an anti-racist lifestyle? Hold onto your mask and snorkel. Let's dive into these crucially important questions.

America has a fixation on racial identity. Immediately after we say a person's name, we add their race. For example, we say, "I just chatted with Luis Sanchez—you know, the Mexican guy in the next block."

And how often have we all heard, "Barack Obama, the first Black president of the United States."

Our nation's preoccupation with race also informs how Americans, including members of the white Church, look at scripture. To this point, Jones notes:

> "White evangelicals have generally claimed that their worldviews and theology are derived directly from a straightforward reading of an inerrant Bible, and thus, by extension, a direct reflection of God's will. But the evidence suggests that it is more accurate to say that white evangelicals, like everyone who engages the text, read their worldview back into the Bible. In human hands, the Bible is as much a screen as a projector."[1]

I am not immune from viewing Scripture through a distorted lens. As I said earlier in the book, I grew up in Jamaica. As a child and teenager, the tropical setting in which I lived influenced my views about the geography of the Bible lands. For example, when I heard or read about 'green pastures' in Psalm 23, I imagined fields of lush, knee-high grass interspersed by shade trees—just like the meadows on my uncle's dairy farm. Later I found out the 'green pastures' of the Bible are somewhat scrubby. Also, I thought the Garden of Gethsemane was as lush as the botanical gardens in Jamaica—with green lawns, bright flowers, leafy shrubs and huge shade trees. Was I wrong!

So, let's remove our filters and discard our prejudices.

Let's take a look at the Bible and see what it *really* says about race. Instead of focusing on race, the Bible focuses on ethnicities. For example, the Bible talks about the Hittites, Canaanites, Philistines—and numerous other ethnic groups ending in ites or ines.

Eight takeaways about race from the Bible[2]

1. Every human being is equal in the sight of God

Genesis 1:26 says that God created humankind in God's own image and likeness. The Bible does not state the race of Adam and Eve. So, we don't know what they looked like. As a result, we are well advised to ignore the depictions in paintings of Eve being a white woman with an hourglass figure and long, straight hair that obscures much of her naked torso. We can deduce that our first parents represented all ethnicities.

God created the first woman and the first man in God's own image and likeness. What does this mean? As opposed to animals, human beings have some mental and spiritual commonalities with God and, as such, can relate to God. Also, God appointed humans as God's representatives on earth. So, every human being—regardless of race—is special, elite and incredibly valuable!

Therefore, anyone who holds the view that his or her race is superior to another race denies the equal status we all have as a human family. Also, consider this: Proverbs 17:5 says, "He who mocks the poor insults his Maker," (RSV). If we mock God when we devalue someone of a lesser economic state, how much more do we insult God when we act in a prejudicial manner to someone of another race?

2. Black Africans were part of ancient Israeli society

A study of the biblical text plus the history of ancient Middle Eastern society reveals that the Israelites included four major ethnic groups:

    a. Semites—including the Israelites, Arameans, Amorites and Canaanites

    b. Indo-Europeans—Philistines and Hittites

    c. Cushites—including Black Africans living south of Egypt along the Nile River (referred to as Ethiopians or Nubians)

    d. Egyptians (Asiatic, North African and African elements)

The patriarch Abraham is widely considered to be the father of the Jewish people and is also highly regarded in the Christian and Islamic religions. Among his descendants were Western Mesopotamians, Canaanites and Egyptians. So, they looked very much like the Semitic peoples of the Middle East today, such as modern Arabs and Israelis. However, during Israel's 400-year sojourn in Egypt, the people of Israel became more diverse—linguistically, culturally and racially. We know this because when God delivered

Israel from Egyptian bondage, the Bible says that, "an ethnically diverse crowd also went up with them" (Exod. 12:38 - HCSB). In all likelihood, this "mixed multitude" as the King James Version of the Bible says, included Black Africans, called Cushites in the text. In fact, Moses married a Cushite woman.

3. God approved of interracial marriage

Moses is widely regarded as one of the most important leaders in Judaism, Christianity and Islam. Numbers 12 records that Moses, who was Jewish, married a Cushite woman. Does Scripture make a big deal about it? Here's what the text says, "Miriam and Aaron spoke against Moses because of the Cushite woman whom he had married." That's it. And the focus of the story is not on the woman's race, but the fact that Moses' sister Miriam and Moses' sidekick Aaron criticized the woman. (Moses' current wife is a different person from Zipporah, a Midianite woman who Moses had married some time earlier.)

But you might ask, didn't God forbid interracial marriage? No. Deuteronomy 7 records that God prohibited the children of Israel from marrying people from the neighboring tribes who worshiped gods other than Jehovah. God says, "You shall not make marriages with them . . . For they would turn away your sons from following me, to serve other gods," (Deut. 7:1-4). So, God's issue was not with people's race, but with peoples' religion.

Did God approve of Moses' marriage to a Black woman? Apparently so. God scolded Miriam and Aaron for opposing the marriage. Miriam was even struck with leprosy over the episode. And Moses and Aaron pleaded with God to heal her. God healed her—after a week of having the affliction.

Here's another huge point. We know from the text that the Israeli people complained a lot. They whined about the journey through the desert. They asked to return to slavery—since they supposedly had better food in servitude. They fussed about the basic ration of manna which God miraculously provided. And while Moses was getting the 10 Commandments from God, they built an idol and danced around it.

But we have no record of the children of Israel objecting to Moses' marriage to an African woman. Maybe that's because interracial liaisons were so commonplace that no one saw it as a big deal! So, we can conclude from these passages that interracial marriage is strongly affirmed by Scripture, provided the marriage is within the faith.

4. God included Black people as part of the tradition of faith

Just before the fall of Jerusalem (about 586 B.C.), Jeremiah the prophet predicted that the Babylonian army would invade Jerusalem. Jeremiah called on the people of Israel to repent and turn back to God. However, the leaders in Jerusalem accused the prophet of treason and stuck him in a cistern—where he would surely die—either through neglect or at the hand of the invaders.

Then, a Cushite man, a North African named Ebed-Melech, asked permission to rescue Jeremiah. Jerusalem fell, and most of the leaders were executed. And God announced that Ebed-Melech would live because he trusted in God and saved Jeremiah (Jer. 39:15-18). The Lord had no issue including people of faith—irrespective of their race or ethnic group—in the list of the faithful!

Shortly after the church was founded, the Bible records the story of the Apostle Phillip leading a man from Ethiopia to faith in Christ. The term used for Ethiopia in the New Testament refers to the same region that 'Cush' refers to in the Old Testament. It is evident from these texts that God wholeheartedly welcomed people of all races and ethnicities into the family of faith.

5. Jesus advocated for multiculturalism and antiracism

Jesus' earthly ministry took place 2,000 years ago in Israel. At that time, Israel was predominantly settled by Jewish people. And the Black-white racial construct that exists in the USA today was not a reality in ancient Israel. As a result, the gospels (Matthew, Mark, Luke and John) do not say a lot about racism per se.

What did Jesus think about how we should view people of different races and cultures? The parable of the Good Samaritan (Luke 10:25-37) gives us a clue. Jesus told the story as an answer to the question from a Jewish guy who asked, "Who is my neighbor?"

The Samaritans were half-Jew and half-Gentile. And most Jewish people considered them to be outcasts. In the parable, a Jewish guy is walking on a lonely road when he gets robbed and beaten up by some bad dudes. A priest and another religious leader pass by and ignore the injured traveler. Then, the Good Samaritan approaches. He gives the beaten-up guy first aid, puts him on his donkey, takes him to a hotel and pays for his stay.

Why did Jesus choose a Samaritan for the story? He wanted to make it abundantly clear that the best way to show neighborliness is to strike up meaningful relationships with people who are the most unlike us. It is conceivable that if Israel had Asians, Native Americans or Blacks, Jesus would have used them for the story. The message is clear: Jesus wants us to accept people of all races and cultures as our neighbors.

6. God deliberately created the Church to be multiracial and multinational

The Book of Acts teaches us that the Church was multiracial and multinational from the beginning. Acts 2 records that about 10 days after Jesus returned to heaven, believers gathered in Jerusalem for the annual Feast of Pentecost. These early believers came from all over the then-known world: Europe, Asia, the Middle East, the Mediterranean—and Africa. They spoke numerous languages and dialects.

God could have chosen any time and place to start the Church. So, it's very significant that God ensured that the Church began as a multinational, multicultural and multilingual body. This means that if our churches are located in multiethnic areas, yet they consist predominantly of one race, we are falling short of the scriptural model!

What's more, John 3:16 says, "For God so loved the world, that He gave His only begotten Son, that whosoever believes in Him should not perish but have everlasting life." The "world" referred to here is the world of every nation, race and ethnic group on the planet!

7. The Apostle Peter models the interracial, intercultural norm of the Church

I believe the clearest evidence in Scripture that people of all races and cultures are accepted by God on an equal basis is the story of Peter. As a leader in the Early Church, Peter was a fearless and effective preacher of the Gospel.

But Peter did not regard non-Jewish people as his equal. Then, God used a series of visions to bring him into contact with a Roman military leader who was a Gentile (Acts 10).

God changed Peter. And here's what he said: "I now realize . . . that God does not show favoritism but accepts from every nation the one who fears him and does what is right," (Acts 10: 34-25).

In other words, God doesn't see skin color or national identities. God sees the heart.

8. The Church in heaven will include people of all races

The Book of Revelation gives us a glimpse of the multiracial makeup of heaven. Revelation 5:9 says that individuals "from every tribe and language and people and nation" (NLT) will worship Christ forever. If God's vision of heaven is to include people from every race, shouldn't we embrace people from every race here on earth, too?

The Bible presents the view that God loves all humans equally—irrespective of race, culture and nationality. Stated differently, no objective reader can find racism in the Bible. That said, millions of white evangelicals are finding innovative ways to explain away Trump's—and their own—racism.

Chapter 4
Is Donald Trump Racist?

Donald Trump is no longer serving as president of the United States. So why do his views on race matter? Because millions of Americans—including Christians—still cling to his every word. And race has been a cornerstone of Trumpism from the get-go. From as early as 2011—five years before the 2016 presidential election—Trump began a campaign questioning whether Barack Obama was born in the United States. (The Constitution stipulates that the president must be US born.) It was well established that Obama was born in Hawaii. But Trump didn't care. He also asserted that Obama was Muslim.[1] Also, when Trump made his now famous 'escalator' announcement about joining the presidential race in 2015, he said, "When Mexico sends its people, they're not sending their best. They're sending people that have lots of problems... They're bringing drugs, they're bringing crime, they're rapists."[2]

Donald Trump is a racist. And every person who cares about justice, human dignity and morality MUST care about Trump's history of racism:[3]

- In 1973, the US Department of Justice sued the Trump Management Corporation for violating the Fair Housing Act. Why? Trump refused to rent to Black tenants. Also, he lied to Black applicants about the availability of apartments.

- In the 1980s, former Trump employee Kip Brown accused one of Trump's businesses of discriminating against Black employees. Brown said that when Trump and his wife Ivana visited the casino, the bosses would order all the Black people off the floor.

- In 1989, five teenagers—four Black and one Latina—were wrongfully accused of raping a white woman jogger in New York City's Central Park. Trump bought full-page ads in local papers demanding that the death penalty be reinstated. After spending 13 years in prison, the teens—now men—were exonerated, based on DNA evidence. Also, the city paid them a $41 million settlement. Yet, in October, 2016, Trump still alleged that the men were guilty.

Is Donald Trump Racist? | 63

- The 1991 book by John O'Donnell, the former president of Trump Plaza Hotel and Casino in Atlantic City, quoted Trump as saying he did not want a Black accountant to count his money. His reason? The man was lazy, and laziness is a trait in Blacks.

- In 1992, the Trump Plaza Hotel and Casino paid a $200,000 fine because the casino moved Black and women dealers off tables to accommodate the prejudices of a gambler.

- During congressional testimony in 1993, Trump said some Native American reservations shouldn't be allowed to operate casinos because the people did not look like Indians to him.

- In 2000, Trump secretly ran a series of ads suggesting the St. Regis Mohawk tribe had a well-documented record of criminal activity. The tribe had proposed opening a casino that could compete with Trump's Atlantic City casino.

- During season two of his TV show, *The Apprentice*, Trump fired Black contestant Kevin Allen for being overeducated.

- Trump publicized false rumors that Barak Obama, America's first Black president, was not born in the USA. Trump also claimed that he sent investigators to Hawaii to check into Obama's birth certificate.

- In 2011, Trump suggested that Obama wasn't a good enough student to have gotten into Columbia University or Harvard Law School.

- In 2015, Trump launched his presidential campaign by calling Mexican immigrants "rapists" who are bringing crime and drugs to the US. He also called for a ban on all Muslims coming into the US.

- In 2016, Trump alleged that Judge Gonzalo Curiel, who was overseeing the Trump University lawsuit, should recuse himself because of the judge's Mexican heritage.

- During the presidential campaign, Trump refused to condemn white supremacists who endorsed him. He also retweeted messages from white supremacists and neo-Nazis.

- Trump repeatedly referred to Sen. Elizabeth Warren (D-MA) as "Pocahontas." He also demeaned her claim, which she later recanted, that she has Native American ancestry.

- During the 2016 Republican convention, Trump positioned himself as the 'law and order' candidate. This was an obvious attempt to allay white fears of Black crime.

- Trump refused to reject the endorsement of David Duke, former grand wizard of the Ku Klux Klan.

- Trump told Black voters in 2016 that they are living in poverty, have terrible schools and have no jobs. "What the hell do you have to lose?" he asked them.

- In the aftermath of the white supremacist protests in Charlottesville, Virginia, in August 2017, Trump said that "both sides" were to blame for the violence and there were "some very fine people" on both sides. This means that to Trump, neo-Nazis are "very fine people."

- In response to African American athletes kneeling during the national anthem in a silent protest against systemic racism, Trump repeatedly called for a range of disciplinary actions against the players, including suspension without pay, being fired on the spot or expulsion from the United States.

- In 2017, Trump said that immigrants from Haiti "probably have AIDS."[4] Trump added that the USA lets everybody into the country and that doing so is "like a death wish for our country." Trump also said that the 40,000 Nigerian visitors would never "go back to their huts" in Africa.[5]

- During a meeting in the White House in January, 2018, Trump raised objections to the USA accepting immigrants from Haiti and African countries. "Why are we having all these people from s***hole countries come here?" he reportedly asked. Trump went on to suggest that the

USA should accept more people from countries like Norway, according to sources at the meeting.[6] The implication? White immigrants are good for the country. Black immigrants are not.

- Trump tweeted that several freshman congresswomen—all women of color—should "go back and help fix the totally broken and crime infested places (countries) from which they came." Trump was referencing Reps. Alexandria Ocasio-Cortez (D-NY), Ayanna Pressley (D-MA), Ilhan Omar (D-MN) and Rashida Tlaib (D-MI). Three of the four congresswomen were born in the USA.

- Trump repeatedly called the COVID-19 virus the "Chinese virus" even though many sources, including the Yale School of Medicine, describe such descriptions as inaccurate, racist and xenophobic.[7] NBC reports that anti-Asian hate crimes increased by nearly 150 percent in 2020, due in part to Trump's "China virus" rhetoric.[8]

- When Kamala Harris was running for Vice President of the United States, Trump unleashed a barrage of attacks against her. He claimed she did not "meet the requirements" for the position, that she was "not competent," that she was "nasty," "disrespectful," "the meanest," "the most horrible" and a "madwoman." Kamala Harris was born in the USA. Her father hailed from Jamaica and her mother from India.[9]

So why does it matter that Trump is a racist? Here are three big reasons: First, Trump's racism is diametrically opposed to the Bible and the teachings of Jesus. So, all followers of Christ should immediately distance themselves from the former president.

Stated differently, one cannot call Christ Lord and follow a racist bigot like Trump!

Second, for white Christians, following Trump and his ideology are an affront to people of color. Trump's racism is so hideous, it should repulse white Christians to the core. I can't deny the Holocaust and be best buddies with Jewish people. I can't kick my dog and expect to serve on the board of the local humane society. And I don't see how any white person can be a true friend to people of color while they follow a man who hates people like me!

Third, Trump's displays of racial hatred foster a culture of hatred for people of color. Experts in managerial science point out that the personal views of a leader affect the corporate culture of the organization he or she leads. This principle applies to organizations from a Boys Scout troupe to the Church, from a corporation to the White House.

As Karen A. Benz, Executive Coach and DISC Facilitator with BetterManager notes:

> "In our experience working with CEOs and C-Suite leaders, they often don't realize how much people in their organizations watch their behavior and decision-making—looking for clues as to what is 'normal.'

Every decision has a ripple effect. And sometimes, that ripple-effect can be extremely harmful."

Benz points out that employees imitate the positive and negative behaviors of their leader. Citing the case of a specific CEO known for being ruthless and sexist, she says,

"His behavior had a trickle-down effect throughout the entire company. Employees think it must be okay to do these things since the CEO is doing them. At the very least, they expect not to be punished for the same behaviors. The result? A discriminating culture against its employees and a culture where sexual harassment was tolerated and, in some cases, encouraged,"[10]

Many media reports point to a big uptick in anti-Black threats, intimidation and acts of violence since Trump became president in 2016. In fact, within weeks after the election, the Southern Poverty Law Center counted more than 200 complaints of hate crimes.[11]

When Trump was vying to become president of the United States, many detractors cited his lying, verbally abusive conduct, history of sexual abuse—and racism—among other complaints, to justify his lack of qualification for the presidency. But many Trump followers, including evangelical leaders, contended that Trump's checkered past did not matter. And others downplayed his racism. One MAGA friend of mine said, "Trump may have said some insensitive things about Mexicans and Black people, but, you know, he really means well, and you can't take everything he says seriously."

God help us!

Chapter 5
The Scourge of Racism in the Church

Christians can't be racist. This was the view I held while growing up in Jamaica. I wasn't naïve. I saw video footage on the evening news of racist people in the American South squirting fire hoses at people of color. I saw images of white police beating Black protesters with batons and of cops handling snarling German Shepherd dogs inches away from the faces of Black citizens.

It wasn't until I moved to America that I found out that white Christians—like white Americans with no faith at all—had 'drank the Kool-Aid' of racial hatred. To my chagrin, I discovered that white missionaries and pastors who spent decades evangelizing people in Africa were as racist as people who hide under white sheets.

Racism as we know it in the Western world is relatively new. Yes, people have hated each other since Cain killed

Abel, as recorded in the book of Genesis. Also, tribes, clans and nations have been warring with other groups from the earliest civilizations. In addition, nations have pressed their enemies into slavery for millennia.

But the discovery of the 'New World' by Christopher Columbus started a new paradigm: the establishment of nations in which white people are predominantly the ruling class and people of color predominantly the servant class. More specifically, the British, Spanish, Dutch and Portuguese led the way in buying or stealing Africans, carting them to the New World in overcrowded, stinking, rat-infested ships and using them as disposable workers.

And the Church found ways to justify this atrocity. Church leaders, along with the ship captains, planters and brokers found ingenious ways to twist Holy Scripture to justify their dastardly deeds. How? They viewed the Bible through a distorted white/Black paradigm in which whites were superior and Black people inferior.

The white Church in America supported white supremacy from the get-go. On Christopher Columbus' second voyage to the West Indies in 1493, he took Conquistadors who helped subjugate the native Indians, including those in present-day Haiti and the Dominican Republic.

The Spanish quelled all resistance from the native people and in effect used them as slaves. In order to keep the native Indians subjugated and free up the Spanish government to keep the profits made from enslaving the Indians, the king of Spain asked for and received permission from

Pope Alexander VI, to 'own' what is present-day North and South America. The king got a total of five papal bulls (similar to public decrees) from the pope.

In the words of *The Popes, the Catholic Church and the Transatlantic Enslavement of Black Africans 1418-1839*, one of these papal bulls "gave the Conquistadors the opportunity to exploit the natives to do the works on their cultivated sugar and cotton plantations as well as to break the hard rocks in order to reach at the gold and silver mines."[1]

However, the natives were not used to doing this kind of work, and thousands of Indians died from hard work and epidemics, such as the flu. The Europeans brought these diseases to the New World, and the Indians had no resistance to them.

This led to the importation of African slaves. And the slave owners raped, beat, tortured and killed Africans by the millions with the blessing of the Church. The white Church in the USA concocted a flawed theology that freed them to own black people. In this regard, Sydney E. Ahlstrom states in his book, *A Religious History of the American People*:

> "That Western Christendom turned Africa into a hunting ground for slaves rather than a field for philanthropic and missionary endeavor in one of the world's tragedies. That the New World became the chief arena for the European exploitation of slave labor is an extension of the same tragedy. That the United States—the first new nation, the elect nation, the nation with the

soul of a church, the great model of modern democracy—moved into the nineteenth century with one of the largest and cruelest of slave systems in its midst with full constitutional protection is surely one of the world's greatest ironies."[2]

In her book, *The Land is Not Empty: Following Jesus in Dismantling the Doctrine of Discovery*, Sarah Augustine calls the stealing of 'yet-to-be-discovered' lands (in the eyes of Europeans) the Doctrine of Discovery. She says, "The Doctrine of Discovery is a theological, philosophical and legal framework dating to the fifteenth century that gave Christian governments moral and legal right to invade and seize Indigenous lands and dominate Indigenous Peoples.[3] She points out that the Doctrine of Discovery is meant to "permanently remove Indigenous Peoples from the birthright of their lands and wealth by force, genocide, relocation, urbanization and forced assimilation."[4]

In *White Too Long*, Robert P. Jones traces the history of white supremacy in the American Church from inception through present-day. Jones' work has to be taken seriously. He is a Southern Baptist who holds a Ph.D. in religion from Emory University and an M.Div. for Southern Baptist Theological Seminary. He is also the founder and CEO of the Public Religion Research Institute.

Jones says, "White Christians churches have not just been complacent; they have not only been complicit; rather, as the dominant cultural power in America, they have been responsible for constructing and sustaining a project to protect white supremacy and resist Black equality."[5]

Indeed, racism is the only institution that has gone through every spiritual movement in American's history unscathed.

Racist theology in the white Church

Slavery by any definition is hideous, cruel and repulsive. However, chattel slavery—such as what was practiced in the Americas, including the United States—was perhaps the most sadistic form of slavery human beings ever practiced on the planet. Chattel slavery allowed people to be considered legal property. As such, slaves could be bought, sold and owned until the day they died. Also, it meant all children born in slavery would be slaves for life. (In rare instances slaves bought their freedom.) In addition, the slave owners had the legal right to abuse their slaves—their property—in any and every conceivable way. So, beatings, rape and the most depraved and sadistic types of torture were all fair game.

This begs the question: How can Christians—people who claim to worship God, who is all loving and the creator of all human beings—justify such a practice? As crude as it sounds, the answer is simple: Create a theology that justifies slavery. And this is exactly what 'Christian' slave owners did. In essence, the justification for slavery went something like this:

God set up a divine order on earth, and different races

and genders have individual roles to play. When everyone fulfills their roles without complaining, all is well. Also, God established the white race to be superior to all others, and the Negro race is naturally subservient to whites. Therefore, enslaving Black people to serve white people is not only justified, it's also key to maintaining the divine order.[6]

Perhaps the biggest justification racist Christians have used to support discrimination and slavery of Black people is citing the 'curse of Ham' in Genesis 9:18-27. The text says that Noah became drunk by drinking wine from his vineyard. He lay naked in his tent. Noah's son, Ham, saw his dad naked and told his two brothers, Shem and Japheth. Shem and Japheth draped a garment between themselves, walked backward into the tent and covered Noah without seeing their dad's nakedness.

When Noah woke up, he learned about the incident and said, "Cursed be Canaan!" (Ham's son). "The lowest of slaves will he be to his brothers." Noah also said, "Praise be to the Lord, the God of Shem! May Canaan be the slave of Shem. May God extend Japheth's territory; may Japheth live in the tents of Shem, and may Canaan be the slave of Japheth," (Genesis 9: 25-27 NIV).

White Christians—including many in the South during the Antebellum period (the years after the War of 1812 and the Civil War)—used this scripture to justify slavery. However, a close examination of the text reveals that these conclusions are farfetched and absurd. In the article, *The Blessing of Whiteness in the Curse of Ham: Reading Gen. 9:18–29 in the Antebellum South,* Wongi Park, Assistant Professor of Religion at Belmont University, Nashville, Tenn., debunks the racist interpretations of the Genesis 9 account.

"The curse is emphatically not uttered by God; it is uttered by a hungover Noah who was perhaps angered at and humiliated by his son," Park says. Also, the punishment of perpetual slavery far outweighs Ham's 'crime' of accidentally or intentionally seeing his father naked.

In addition, the Genesis text does not support the notion that the sons of Noah represent the genesis of Mongolian, Caucasian and Negro races as adherents to the 'curse of Ham' theory believe. Such a take on the naked Noah story is all speculation. In fact, there is no scientific evidence supporting the position that the three major racial groups have their genesis in Noah's three sons.

The idea advanced by Christian white supremacists that the descendants of Shem, Ham and Japheth ultimately became the predominant races to occupy Asia, Africa and Europe respectively is also nonsensical. There is zero anthropological or historical support for such a notion. In fact, Park makes the case that nothing in the Genesis text connotes skin color. The term used for Ham in many standard Hebrew lexicons, refers to "heat or warmth" (Genesis 8:22; Jeremiah 17:8; Job 24:19). It also refers to hot bread in Joshua 9:12 and 1 Samuel 21:7. Park says:

"Ham is not Black. He is therefore made Black or 'blackened' into existence in and through the racist antebellum interpretation. Similarly, the notion of whiteness as color, race or ethnicity is absent in the text of Genesis 9:18-29. Japheth is not white. He is made white through the racist antebellum interpretation."[7]

The result of this racist theology is that the white Church has been able to justify a two-tiered system in which whites are the ruling class and Blacks and other people of color, the working class. The white Church has kept white supremacy alive and vibrant in part through this bigoted interpretation of Holy Scripture.

In this regard, Jones notes that Christian theology and institutions in America have consistently supported white supremacy. He observes:

"A close examination of the key theological doctrines such as the Christian worldview of salvation, the centrality of a personal relationship with Jesus, and the use of the Bible reveals how each was tailored to resist Black equality and protect white supremacy, and how this legacy dramatically limits the moral and religious vision of white Christianity today."[8]

A sordid history of white supremacy in the Church

The Southern Baptist Convention is the largest evangelical Christian denomination in the USA. As such, the church is a barometer of racist attitudes in the white Church in America.

The Southern Baptist Convention was formed in May 1845 over the issue of slavery. More specifically, the Baptists in the South broke with their counterparts in the North over whether slaveowners could be sent out as missionaries. (The Northern Baptists said no, while the Southern Baptists said yes.)[9]

In fact, the Southern Baptists supported slavery, the Confederacy and the succession of the South from the United States of America.[10] In addition, the Southern Baptist Theological Seminary was founded in 1859 by white supremacists who raised funds through their slave holdings.

After the Civil War, which the South lost, the Southern Baptist Convention played an influential role in Southern culture. In fact, by the middle of the 20th century, the Southern Baptists pretty much set the tone for much of American Christianity.

Many of the influential leaders in the Christian world were and are Southern Baptists. Popular Southern Baptists church/Christian leaders (past and present) include Chuck Colson (1931–2012) Founder of Prison Fellowship and author; Jerry Falwell (1933–2007) pastor, televangelist, Liberty University founder; Billy Graham (1918-2018) evangelist; Franklin Graham, CEO Samaritan's Purse; Mike Huckabee, Southern Baptist Minister and former governor of Arkansas and 2016 Republican presidential candidate; Robert Jeffress, pastor of First Baptist Church in Dallas, Texas; David Jeremiah, pastor of Shadow Mountain Community Church, El Cajon, Calif.; Thom S. Rainer, former President and CEO Life Way Christian Resources in Nashville, Tenn.; Charles F. Stanley (1932-2023), Pastor Emeritus First Baptist Church of Atlanta, Ga.; and Rick Warren, pastor of the Saddleback Church, Calif.

Prior to and during the Civil War, many white Christians in the North took issue with their counterparts in the South concerning slavery. However, after the Civil War, the white Christians who opposed slavery failed to take real steps toward equality with their Black brothers and sisters. As a result, the white-equals-superiority, Black-equals-inferiority model prevailed in the Church. Also, white Christians participated in a raft of horrific acts to reinforce white superiority—particularly in the South.

One of the most horrific examples of the complicity of white Christians in race-related violence took place in the spring of 1899. Samuel Thomas Wilks was a Black Georgia farmhand who was accused of murdering a prominent white planter named Alfred Cranford. White area newspapers claimed that Wilks brutally murdered Cranford, yanked an infant from Cranford's wife's arms and raped the wife. Wilks, who was on the run, claimed that he killed Cranford in self-defense and that he did not rape Mrs. Cranford.

On the day following the crime, the *Atlanta Constitution* ran a sensational story calling for the lynching of Wilks. The governor of Georgia and the newspaper each posted a $500 reward for the capture of Wilks. An angry mob started searching for the wanted man.

He was finally caught on a Sunday morning, and word

spread quickly around Atlanta and the surrounding area. Christians by the thousands poured out of the churches in Atlanta and hurried onto specially organized trains to the small town of Newnan, just southwest of Atlanta. Meanwhile a mob sprung Wilks from the jail, paraded him through the town and led him to a field just outside the town. There, Wilkes was stripped naked, severely tortured, doused with kerosene and burned. His last words were "Sweet Jesus!" At every stage, thousands of white Christians, who had just got out of church, cheered.[11]

Such was the depravity of white racism in the Church!

Many white evangelical churches made a habit of excluding people of color from attending church services. Consider the unspeakably meanspirited actions of Allen Thompson, mayor of Jackson and a well-known member of the Galloway Memorial United Methodist Church in Jackson, Miss. In 1963, Thompson convinced the city council to pass a resolution that in effect made it a crime for a person of color to set foot into the church. The offender could be hit with a fine up to $500 and as much as six months in the slammer. And, yes, Black worshippers and the white people who invited them were carted off from church—to jail![12]

In 1963, Civil Rights activist Medgar Evans and a white chaplain were prohibited from entering the First Baptist Church in Galloway, Miss. Some weeks later, Evans—a husband and father of three small children—was gunned down in his driveway. The assailant was Bryon De La Beckwith Jr. It's bad enough that Beckwith was a member of the White Citizens' Council in Greenwood. But even worse, he was also a member in good standing of the Greenwood Episcopal Church of the Nativity.[13]

This trend of exclusion from worship services led to the birth and growth of Black denominations in America. In this regard, Benjamin Quarles observes in his book, *The Negro in the Making of America*: "The emergence of the all-Negro church resulted in part from an unwillingness by colored communicants to worship in seats reserved for them in the rear of the church or in the gallery."[14]

Some white churches permitted blacks to attend services, but they had to sit in a separate section away from the white parishioners. The African Methodist Episcopal Church was born as a result of such segregated services. The church was founded by Richard Allen, who was born in slavery in 1760 and purchased his freedom at age 21. Allen joined the Methodist church and became an itinerant preacher in places like New York and South Carolina. Allen returned to his hometown of Philadelphia and joined St George's Methodist Episcopal Church. There, he served as a preacher to the Black parishioners.

The church forced Black worshippers to sit in a balcony overlooking the main sanctuary. One Sunday morning, Allen and several other Black members were on their knees praying when a white sextant ordered them to stop praying immediately and move to another section. In disgust, Allen and about 40 other Black worshippers walked out of the church, never to return.

The group rented a room for worship services, but St. George's Church threatened to excommunicate them from the Methodist Church if they kept meeting separately. Since Allen and his group treasured membership in the Methodist denomination, they hated the prospect of being 'read out of the church.' In fact, the group challenged the leadership at St. George's to show them where they had violated any of the church's laws. St. George's found no such violations but kept threatening to expunge the Black Christians from membership.

In the interim, Allen and the other leaders raised money to build a new house of worship. Ultimately, Allen and a group of supporters bought an unused building on Sixth Street in Philadelphia and renovated it to become their new church, which they called Bethel Church. However, the Methodist Church perpetually placed stumbling blocks in the way of the Black church remaining part of the Methodist denomination. For example, a letter was distributed that disavowed Bethel Church from being considered Methodists. The white Methodists also started a new church in the neighborhood and encouraged Bethel members to attend there. One prominent Methodist elder even insisted on preaching at Bethel and taking spiritual charge of the congregation.

Allen and his cohorts found out that bourgeoning Black churches in other cities were experiencing similar struggles with breaking free from white control. This led to a conference in April 1816, in which delegates came from Baltimore and other cities. The Black churches decided to become one denomination under the name African Methodist Episcopal Church.[15]

So, the AME church did not come about as a result of theological differences (such as regarding the Bible, God, the Trinity, the personal and work of Christ, the sacraments or eschatology). Rather, the AME church was born because of white supremacy!

Meanwhile, the white Church in the South worked in tandem with local government to reinforce their white supremacy. In 1954, the Supreme Court ruled (in Brown v. Board of Education) that racial segregation in public schools was unconstitutional. Many Protestant denominations officially approved the ruling. Yet, as Jones observes, "the Mississippi State Legislature moved quickly to protect the ability of local white churches to oppose their national offices and remain segregated, while still retaining their property."[16]

Given the terrible treatment Black people received at the hand of white Christians in America over the years, it's not surprising that many Black Americans held white Christians in low esteem. The views of Frederick Douglass provide an insight into this matter. An escaped slave, Douglass became an abolitionist, orator, writer and statesman. He claimed that Christian slaveowners were more cruel to their slaves than non-Christian slave owners. Douglass spoke from personal experience. His former owner, Thomas Auld in Maryland, converted to Christianity while Douglass was his slave.

In his book, *Narrative of the Life of Frederick Douglass*, the former slave said, "Were I to be again reduced to the chains of slavery, next to that enslavement, I should regard being the slave of a religious master the greatest calamity that could befall me. For of all slaveholders with whom I have ever met, religious slaveholders are the worst. I have ever found them to be meanest and bassest, the most cruel and cowardly of all others. It was my unhappy lot not only to belong to a religious slaveholder, but to live in a community of such religionists."[17]

Douglass based this conclusion on the observation that Christian slave owners used their faith as an excuse to be harsher than their non-Christian counterparts. Speaking of Auld, his former owner, Douglass said, "Prior to his conversion, he relied upon his own depravity to shield and sustain him in his savage barbarity; but after his conversion, he found religious sanction and support for his slaveholding cruelty,"[18]

The defeat of the Southern Confederacy in 1865—with the resultant end of slavery—left many white Christians in a theological dilemma, in addition to their economic downfall. If owning slaves was part of God plan for their 'esteemed' white race, what is God expecting them to do now? Historians call this trend The Lost Cause. In essence, the Lost Cause is a fictional take on the Civil War, in which the cause of the Confederate states was just, heroic and not centered on slavery. As such, the Confederate defeat is viewed in the best possible light."[19]

White Christians in the South for the most part retained their white supremacist views after emancipation. However, they drummed up a variety of explanations for losing their legal right to enslave Black people. Some asserted that they had failed to be the caliber of slave owners that they should have been. As a result, their defeat was a form of punishment. Others took the opposing view. They held that the Union's victory had nothing to do with righteousness. Therefore, subjugating and enslaving Negroes was still morally prudent.[20]

Many white Christians viewed the defeat of the Southern plantocracy through an eschatological lens. Their defeat was only temporary, they argued, and they will ultimately be exonerated—similar to Christ's death and future resurrection. Also, they held that chattel slavery itself will one day rise again.[21]

Prior to the Civil War, most white evangelicals in the South held a postmillennialist view. According to this view, the world is getting increasingly 'Christian'—as exemplified in the establishment of the Confederacy. Christ will return, according to this view, when the 'civilized,' 'Christian' nation reaches its apex.

When this Confederacy was lost, however, this view also lost its appeal. This led many white evangelicals to gravitate toward a premillennialist view. In essence, this view presents the world as sliding deeper and deeper into moral and spiritual decay. According to this view, Christ will return at any moment and will take all the redeemed to heaven and then establish a righteous reign on earth.[22]

White evangelicals in the South used the premillennialist view as an excuse to relax any commitment to social justice—including any attempts at antiracism. The prevailing view went something like this: Since the world is becoming increasingly godless anyway, it's futile to try to fix it. Rather, Christians should focus on saving souls.[23]

The failure of white evangelicals to radically address the matter of race prejudice didn't end with proponents of the Lost Cause. *Politico* reports that the late evangelist Billy Graham "was missing in action when it came to civil rights legislation." In his landmark 'I Have a Dream Speech' of 1963, King spoke of a "beloved community" in which "little Black boys and little Black girls will join hands with little white boys and white girls." Graham dismissed that dream as utopian. "Only when Christ comes again will the little white children of Alabama walk hand in hand with little Black children," he said.[24]

Ironically, however, some Christians who were abolitionists before the Civil War supported racial segregation after the war. The famous revivalist evangelist Charles Finney is an example. Finney wrote a letter to a close friend who supported integrated seating in their church. Finney told his friend that slavery was "a direct and outrageous violation of fundamental right." However, he contended that race prejudice—hence segregated seating in church—was okay since it "does not necessarily deprive any man of any positive right."[25]

Throughout the period of racial segregation in the United States, white churches and institutions kept on defending segregation and practicing white supremacy. And to a lesser or greater degree, this practice continues to this day.

Another sphere in which the white Church in America practiced white supremacy was toward Native Americans. Between the 19th and 20th centuries, Catholic and Protestant denominations in the USA operated more than 150 boarding schools across the country.[26] In these schools, Native American and Alaskan Native children were separated from their tribal families in order to become Christianized—and 'civilized.' As a result, Native American kids were forced to trade their native religion for Christianity, their native language for English and their cultural practices (such as hunting, dance, interpersonal relationships and hierarchical system) for European models.[27]

Abuses abounded. According to estimates by the Truth and Reconciliation Commission in Canada, some 3,200 Native children in North America died in boarding schools over a 120-year period. In addition, the commission found 31,907 verified cases of assault or sexual abuse. During one hearing, a Native American Chief said that a large amount of fur garments and boots were sent to one school by native parents. (Of course, Canadian winters are colder than winters in the lower 48.) The lovingly made items, given to protect the precious children, were burned. The reason? They were made by 'savages.'[28]

In recent years, the Catholic Church and several evangelical denominations have apologized to Native American over their past racist behavior toward Native peoples. Yet, white supremacy by Christians in America persists to this day—and might even be getting a boost by Trumpism.

Chapter 6
White Supremacy in the Trump Era

It has been more than a century since slavery was abolished in the United States, more than a half century since the Civil Rights Era and half a decade since an African American, Barack Obama, served as president. And we are well into the second decade of the 21st century. Does this mean that white Christians in America have moved beyond their racist attitudes toward people of color?

Apparently not. The Public Religion Research Institute conducted numerous opinion research surveys using the latest tools and techniques in the industry. Survey after survey concludes that overall, white evangelical Christians are far more racist than white Catholics or white Americans who do not claim to have any particular faith. Here are some examples:

- On 'taking a knee': While 72 percent of white Christians believe that professional athletes should be mandated to stand during the national anthem before a game, only 34 percent of people with no religious affiliation and 21 percent of African American Protestants believe this.[1]

- On using race as an excuse for economic inequities: A full 83 percent of white evangelicals "believe that racial minorities use racism as an excuse for economic inequities more than they should." In contrast, 52 percent of religiously unaffiliated whites and 30 percent of Black Protestants do."[2]

- On building a wall on the US/Mexico border: Two out of three white evangelicals Christians in American support Trump's plan to build a wall along the US-Mexican border, while relatively few religiously unaffiliated people do.[3]

Without a doubt, the most flagrant display of white supremacy that occurred during Trump's four-year tenure took place in Charlottesville, Va., August 11-12, 2017. Hundreds of white supremacists converged on Charlottesville to protest the removal of Confederate monuments in Charlottesville and other locations in the South.

The marchers represented several white supremacist groups including neo-fascists, neo-Nazis and members of far-right militias and the Ku Klux Klan. As peaceful counter-protesters watched, the marchers carried symbols of divisiveness and hate including Confederate battle flags plus KKK and Nazi icons.[4]

During the two-day event, protesters repeated some ominous slogans and chants that indicated their racist ideologies and violent intent. The incantations included, "Russia is our friend" and "The South will rise again."

As I saw the protest unfold in real time on my TV screen, it occurred to me that some of the chants were downright scary. One chant said, "You will not replace us!" This chant reflects the fears among white nationalists that the white way of life in America is under attack from nonwhite people who will ultimately outnumber white Americans, thereby 'replacing' them. Along the same lines, some of the marchers yelled the antisemitic sentiment, "Jews will not replace us!"

Other marchers chanted the bone-chilling line, "Blood and soil!" The slogan is a throwback to Nazi Germany and was used by ruthless nationalists who advocated antisemitism and Adolf Hitler's quest to expand Germany into neighboring countries occupied by Germans. White nationalists also chanted "White lives matter," a reference to the Black Lives Matter movement, and an obvious reference to advancing white supremacy. Perhaps the most telling chant was "Hail Trump!" The meaning is obvious: Trump, like Hitler, is the leader of white nationalists and the chanters are looking to Trump to deliver white power and control at all costs.[5]

Predictably, counter protesters clashed with the white nationalists, resulting in local and state police responding in riot gear. Virginia Gov. Terry McAuliffe declared a state of emergency. Yet, the violence got deadly. A white nationalist drove his car into a group of counter protesters, killing a woman and injuring 35 other people.

By this time, the protests were being broadcast on live television, and many people within and outside the government called on Trump to condemn the white nationalist agitators. Trump refused to do so. He made an initial statement, condemning the "display of hatred, bigotry, and violence on many sides." He later said that there were "very fine people on both sides."

Anyone with moral convictions—let along biblical convictions—would readily condemn white supremacists who advocate violence against Jews and people of color—not to mention ramming a car into protesters. But not Trump. At the very least, he established a moral equivalency between white supremacists and citizens who believe in racial equality. But a more accurate explanation is that he welcomed the support of the most hateful fringe groups in America. And they are such an integral part of his base, that he refuses to distance himself from them.[6]

This begs the question: How can people who claim to follow Jesus support a leader who turns a blind eye to white supremacy, antisemitism and violence?

Despite being more racist than white people who are religiously unaffiliated, white evangelical Christians in America think of themselves as having warm feelings about African Americans. However, these same white Christians hold racist attitudes toward people of color.[7] This explains the practice of white churches financially supporting mission efforts among Black and Brown people in the United States and overseas while still being racist. Take my former megachurch as a case in point. The church supports missionary outreaches in places like India, Kenya, Haiti, Jamaica and Honduras. Their support includes hosting delegations from these countries and sending teams to assist with construction projects, medical work and the like. Each year, the church hosts a massive feeding drive in which thousands of church members—children through senior citizens—plus members of the community fill thousands of bags with nutritious grains that are then sent to needy people around the globe.

Some members of my 'small church' participated in these programs. Yet, not one of them expressed an ounce of empathy when I expressed concern about the safety of my son and son-in-law at the hand of racist white police officers.

In addition, Pastor Greg routinely makes digs at Black and Brown countries in his sermon illustrations. In one case, he was preaching a sermon about the benefits of Christians who are older and/or more mature in the faith mentoring 'younger' pastors. He told stories about how other Midwestern pastors supported him earlier in his ministry.

Then, Pastor Greg said that one older minister in his denomination took him on a trip to Haiti to 'widen' his experiences. "You should see the size of the rats there!" he joked. The sounds of laughter rippled through the sanctuary.

I resisted the urge to stand to my feet and protest the insensitive and racist dig at a country that's a neighbor of Jamaica in the Caribbean Sea. Certainly, there were negative aspects to the stories about Pastor Greg's mentorship experiences among white people stateside. But Greg did not tell those stories. Yet, he had to make a cheap jab at Haiti—and elicit laughter from the 99 percent white audience at the expense of Haitians. Would pastor Greg have made that comment if the Haitians were present in the room?

Pastor Greg's joke about the rats in Haiti was not a spur-of-the-moment comment. Greg repeated the same racist, insensitive comment in all three sermons he gave that Sunday morning! (I checked the recordings.) Also, the sermon is broadcast on a wider audience on the Internet. As soon as I returned home, I told Pastor Greg via email that I resented the racist comment. He did not respond. I spoke to him on several occasions since sending the email, but he did not mention my email.

On another occasion, Pastor Greg told a story about how he was late for a flight back to the USA from a third-world country. So, he got into a taxi and demanded that the driver speed to the airport. For some reason, the driver drove slower that Pastor Greg wanted or expected. So, Greg told the congregation what he said to the taxi driver, "What part of hurry don't you understand?" Again, the 99 percent white congregation laughed. I did not. I wondered why Greg thought he had the right to berate a dark-skinned taxi driver because he, Greg, was late in getting to the airport.

A comment like, "Could you drive a bit faster, please? I am running late for my flight," would have sufficed. But, no! Greg had to be the in-your-face white American, rudely making demands of people of color. In my decade of being part of the megachurch, I have never heard Pastor Greg make an insensitive comment about any white person or white country!

Evangelical churches are where people hear the Good News about Jesus' love for all the people of the world. I cannot count the number of times I heard John 3:16 quoted:

> "For God so loved the world, that He gave His only begotten Son, that whosoever believeth in Him should not perish, but have everlasting life" (KJV).

The preacher would stop at the word, "whosoever," to make the point that Christ loves the world so much that people of all races, classes and degrees of sinfulness are equally deserving of God's forgiveness.

Also, in Sunday school, children are taught the *Jesus Loves the Little Children* song. The first verse goes like this:

> "Jesus loves the little children
> All the children of the world
> Red and yellow, Black and white
> They are precious in His sight
> Jesus loves the little children of the world."

So, is it fair to assume that going to church more frequently in America makes people less racist? Apparently not. As Jones points out:

> "There is a positive relationship between holding racist attitudes and white Christian identity among *both* frequent (weekly or more) and infrequent (seldom or never) church attenders. And for white evangelical Protestants, holding racist views has nearly four times the power to predict the likelihood of identification among frequent church attenders than among infrequent church attenders."[8]

This statistic is disturbing. But it gets worse. Jones notes that if one were recruiting for a white supremacist cause on a Sunday morning, "You'd likely have more success hanging out in the parking lot of an average white Christian church—evangelical Protestant, mainline Protestant or Catholic—than approaching whites sitting out services at the local coffee shop."[9]

As the saying goes, you can't make this stuff up!

Chapter 7

Key to Developing an Antiracist Culture

In 1968, Dr. Martin Luther King Jr. wrote, "It is appalling that the most segregated hour of Christian America is eleven o-clock on Sunday morning . . . Equally appalling is the fact that the most segregated school of the week is the Sunday school."[1] Sadly, Dr. King's words are as apt today as when he first said them more than 60 years ago.

Jesus said, "I will build my church, and the gates of Hades will not overcome it" (Matthew 19:18, NIV). Jesus did not say he will build a white Church, a Black Church or a Church for each nationality and ethnic group under heaven. Every believer on planet earth belongs to the same Church—the multinational, multicultural, multilingual Church God created at Pentecost, as recorded in Acts 2.

So, any local church that supports racial divisions in any form is a church that's outside the will of God. Yet, as we illustrated in the previous chapters, the white Church in America is as divided as ever. What's the solution? We need to transition from a racist Church to a Church that fully embraces people of all races and cultures—a fully antiracist Church. We're now in the 21st century. And as a Church, we have fallen short of God's ideal concerning racism for far too long.

Before we start on the road to antiracism, we need to understand the dynamics of racism. And this journey begins with an understanding of white privilege.

The malady of white privilege

White privilege is a term some white supremacists would love to remove from the lexicon. When my former pastor, Greg, said he do not find the term 'white privilege' helpful, I asked, "Have you read what experts, including Peggy McIntosh, have said on the matter?"

"I don't have time to read," he responded.

Then it dawned on me: As one who benefits from white privilege, Pastor Greg can easily live in a fool's paradise and deny the existence of white privilege. But that does not make it disappear. Unlike Pastor Greg, millions of Black and Brown Americans experience the ugly reality of white privilege and Black oppression on a daily basis.

A *Washington Post* article points out that Black Americans account for less than 13 percent of the U.S. population, "but are killed by police at more than twice the rate of white

Americans." The article also notes that "Hispanic Americans are also killed by police at a disproportionate rate."[2]

George Floyd didn't know his Black skin would seal his fate when he walked into a convenience store in Minneapolis, Minn., on May 25, 2020. Floyd chatted and laughed with shoppers and store employees as he walked around the store. He bought a banana. Then, he approached the cashier and attempted to buy a box of cigarettes with a $20 bill. Christopher Martin, the cashier, accepted the bill, even though he thought it might be fake. The young cashier also suspected that Floyd was intoxicated or high on drugs. (It turns out, he had low levels of fentanyl and methamphetamine in his system.) Floyd left the store and returned to his SUV parked outside.

Martin alerted his manager about the possibility that the bill was fake. Then, on two occasions, Martin returned to the SUV and asked Floyd to return to the store and talk to the manager to resolve the issue. Floyd refused to do so. Martin said he offered to pony up the 20 bucks, but the manager had an assistant call 911.[3]

When the police arrived, they forcibly removed Floyd from his SUV, shoved him into the back of a police vehicle and informed him that he was under arrest for passing counterfeit money. The 6' 4" former bouncer told the cops that he was claustrophobic and couldn't breathe. The struggle continued, and the officers yanked Floyd from the SUV and threw him onto the street. While there, white police officer Derek Chauvin kneeled on George Floyd's neck for 9 long minutes and 29 seconds, killing him.

Five years earlier, Dylann Roof, a 21-year-old white supremacist, stepped into a Bible study taking place at Emanuel African Methodist Episcopal Church in Charleston, South Carolina. Roof opened fire on the group of Black worshipers, slaughtering nine of them. The victims included senior pastor, Rev. Clementa Pinckney, who was also a civil rights activist and state senator.[4]

Roof had already posted white supremacy symbols on his website. He also posted a manifesto in which he expressed his hatred for Black people and Jews. After the mass murder, Roof went on the run. He was captured the next day 250 miles north of Charleston. By this time, Roof was very hungry. So, a police officer went to a Burger King and bought a burger for the white mass murderer. Roof was never struck, beaten or physically abused in any way. Instead, he received service with a smile.[5]

A Black man murdered over a fake $20 bill and a white mass murderer arrested without incident and given a yummy hamburger!

Not long ago, I saw a social media post that showed the faces of Black and white men arrested for murder. Typical of mug shots, all of the young men looked sad. However, there was a marked difference between white faces and the Black faces. All the white murder suspects had unblemished faces. However, every single Back face was grotesquely distorted—swollen eyes, fat lips, bumps and bruises on the forehead, cheeks and chin.

This, ladies and gentlemen, is a portrait of white privilege in America today! White Christians cannot fully understand racism, let alone move along the continuum toward antiracism until they come to terms with white privilege!

I could cite tons of data which clearly illustrate that white Americans are granted benefits and privileges at a rate that outstrip people of color. But instead, I have chosen to illustrate my point by using the journalistic mantra, 'If it bleeds, it leads.' Because these incidents serve as a barometer of other acts of white privilege that are largely obscured from public view.

White privilege is alive and well in America society and in the Church as well. *Merriam-Webster* defines white privilege as a "set of social and economic advantages that white people have by virtue of their race."[6] Peggy McIntosh, Senior Research Scientist of the Wellesley Centers for Women in Massachusetts, had done some landmark work in the area of white privilege.

An antiracist activist, scholar and speaker, McIntosh is the founder of the National SEED Project on Inclusive Curriculum. In 1988, she published the article *White Privilege and Male Privilege: A Personal Account of Coming to See Correspondences Through Work in Women's Studies.* She also published the piece, *White Privilege: Unpacking the Invisible Knapsack.* McIntosh defines white privilege as "An invisible package of unearned assets that I can count on cashing in each day. White privilege is like an invisible weightless knapsack of special provisions, assurances, tools, maps, guides, codebooks, passports, visas, clothes, compass, emergency gear and blank checks."

She adds: "I did not earn (the special circumstances and conditions of white privilege) but I have been made to feel (they) are mine by birth, by citizenship, and by virtue of being a conscientious law-abiding 'normal' person of goodwill." [7]

The privileges of being white extend beyond economic benefits. Indeed, the privileges make whiteness a wall that establishes Anglo-Saxons as exceptional compared to people on the other side of this whiteness.[8] The Trump presidency is the quintessential example of white privilege. As African-American Episcopal priest Rev. Kelly Delaine Brown Douglas states:

> The truth is this country, even as it proclaims freedom and justice for all, was founded on an 'Anglo-Saxon myth' of white racial superiority. This is a truth that Donald Trump's politics has tapped into and brought into clear relief. Simply put, during his campaign and ... presidency, Mr. Trump guilefully exploited America's defining Anglo-Saxon myth while dangerously revitalizing the culture of whiteness that serves to protect it.[9]

Here are four key factors about white privilege:

1. White privilege gives white people unearned freedoms and protects people when they exercise those freedoms

Lifestyle choices and a host of daily routines that are normal and natural for white people are often unattainable for people of color. Stated differently, white people are able to do things and get away with them in ways that people of color are not allowed to do. Rather than discuss evidence of white privilege in the 'old' days of the 1950s and 60s, I will give some more recent examples:

- Donald Trump routinely gets into angry tirades while making speeches. He brags about abusing women. He lies incessantly. He bullies his political adversaries in the most outlandish manner. He vilifies his opponents. He sides with Russia and other adversaries. He eviscerates Presidents Biden and Obama, Hillary Clinton and others. Yet, no one attributes his vile, raucous conduct to his race or upbringing.

- As soon as prominent people of color voice opposition to Trump, he draws attention to their race, ethnicity or religion. For example, four Democratic freshman congresswomen who initially comprised the liberal group called The Squad, have met the ire of Trump and other members of the Republican party. The women are Alexandria Ocasio-Cortez (called AOC), a Latina; Ilhan Omar, Somalia-born; Ayanna Pressley, African American; and Rashida Tlaib, Palestinian descent—and Muslim. Trump tweeted that the 'Squad' is "a very racist group of troublemakers who are young, inexperienced, and not very smart." He also said that the women should "go back" to where they came from. All four women are US citizens, and only one was born outside the USA. Trump also tweeted that the lawmakers are incapable of "loving our country." Since all four women are US citizens, the USA belongs to them as much as it does to Trump.

Another blatant example of white privilege is the saga of Kyle Rittenhouse. As a 17-year-old white vigilante from Antioch, Ill., Rittenhouse responded to calls on the Internet for 'patriots' who were willing to take up arms and 'protect' businesses in Kenosha, Wis. Protests had broken out in that city, just north of the Illinois state line, following the shooting of Jacob Blake, an unarmed African American man.

In Kenosha, Rittenhouse armed himself with a spanking new AR-15-style rifle which a friend illegally purchased for him. (Rittenhouse was too young to own the rifle.)[10] A wannabe medic, Rittenhouse also took some first aid supplies with him. Rittenhouse was a certified lifeguard trained in CPR, defibrillator use and 'basic life support.'[11] Some protesters began pursuing Rittenhouse. One of them was Joseph Rosenbaum, a 36-year-old unarmed Kenosha man who had a history of drug abuse, mental problems and incarceration.

Rosenbaum threw a plastic bag at Rittenhouse. Then, Rosenbaum also tried to take Rittenhouse's rifle from him. Rittenhouse pumped four bullets into the unarmed man, killing him on the spot. Rittenhouse then ran down the street and was pursued by protesters who witnessed the shooting.[12]

Body count: One dead.

One of the protesters chasing Rittenhouse was a 26-year-old skateboarder, Anthony Huber. With skateboard in hand, Huber caught up with Rittenhouse and hit him with the skateboard, in an attempt to stop the young vigilante. A scuffle ensued, and Rittenhouse fired a round into Huber's heart, killing him.[13]

Body count: 2 dead.

As Rittenhouse lay on the ground, a 26-year-old man, Gaige Grosskreutz, approached him. A licensed gun owner, Grosskreutz, pointed his Glock pistol at Rittenhouse, under the guise that he feared for his life. Rittenhouse discharged his AR-15-style weapon once again, blowing away most of Grosskreutz' right biceps.

Body count: 2 dead, one injured.

The next day, Rittenhouse was arrested at his home in Illinois. His charges included two counts of first-degree intentional homicide, which carry a sentence of life in prison. Other charges included attempted homicide for shooting the skateboarder and recklessly endangering the safety of a video journalist, Richard McGinnis. Rittenhouse also chalked up a misdemeanor charge for possessing a weapon as a minor.[14] If the young shooter was found guilty of all charges, he would face several hundred years in prison.

The treatment Rittenhouse received the night of the shooting and subsequently represents a classic case of white privilege. At 17 years old, Rittenhouse could not legally carry an assault rifle. But he did so anyway, and he was not confronted by law enforcement. In fact, Rittenhouse testified that several law enforcement officers thanked him for helping to 'protect' the community. Would the police in Kenosha have allowed an equally armed Black or Latino kid to roam around during a curfew? I think not.

After shooting three people, Rittenhouse approached the police with his hands in the air. He was followed by protesters who shouted that Rittenhouse had killed people. However, the police did not arrest Rittenhouse at the scene. Pep Moretti, a white police officer, testified that he did not arrest Rittenhouse on the spot because he could still hear active gunfire.[15] This explanation makes absolutely no sense. By Officer Moretti's logic, only one shooter at a time can be active during a massive protest. And like the adage goes, if you believe Officer Moretti's account, I have a bridge to sell you.

Rittenhouse did not land on the moon. Nor did he cure cancer or negotiate world peace. Rather, he killed two men and injured another with an illegally obtained assault rifle during a curfew. In fact, police later charged Rittenhouse with a curfew violation.[16] Yet, right-wing extremists, the right-wing media and members of the Republican party treated the shooter like a folk hero.

In short order, crowdfunding websites and other sources, including former Silver Spoons child actor Ricky Schroder and MyPillow Inc. founder Mike Lindell poured $2 million dollars into a defense fund for the Kenosha vigilante. Prosecutors alleged that Rittenhouse flashed a white power sign while in a Wisconsin bar following his arraignment.[17] The trial resulted in Rittenhouse being found innocent on all charges. The charges of curfew violation and the charge of possession of a dangerous weapon by a person under 18 were dismissed. In his closing argument, lead prosecutor Thomas Binger told the jury, "You cannot claim self-defense against a danger you create. If you're the one threatening others, you lose the right to claim self-defense."[18] The jury rejected Binger's argument and agreed to render a verdict of not guilty on all counts.

Fox News hailed Rittenhouse as the real victim. In an appearance on Fox & Friends, Fox News' Tucker Carlson claimed that the three men who clashed with Rittenhouse were "all convicted felons who are trying to kill him." Joseph Rosenbaum has an arrest record. The others didn't.

Ignoring the fact that Rittenhouse traveled 30 miles from Antioch, Ill., to Kenosha, Wis., Carlson said, "Here was a kid who was trying to help his own community."

And although Rittenhouse strutted into town as a wannabe cop with an assault-style rifle, Carlson adds, "He defends himself and he is charged with murder."[19] But why should anyone be surprised? This is Fox News. So, truth be damned!

Donald Trump hosted Kyle Rittenhouse at the former president's Mar-a-Lago estate in Florida and found Rittenhouse to be "really a nice young man."[20] Also, prominent

Republican lawmakers—including Reps. Matt Gaetz of Florida and Paul Gosar of Arizona—expressed interest in hiring Rittenhouse as an intern. However, Rittenhouse's lawyer Mark Richards called those offers "disgusting" and said the Congress members made the offers in order to raise money on Rittenhouse.[21]

In a front-page article following the announcement of the Rittenhouse not-guilty verdict, the *Huntington News*, the independent newspaper of Northeastern University, published an article which placed the verdict as part of the continuum of white vigilantism in America. "White vigilantism is central in American history," the article says. In reference to Rittenhouse and other vigilantes, the article notes:

> "Rather than defending property . . . these white vigilantes were looking for violence. With the high-profile Rittenhouse case enabling these wannabe police officers to act violently without impudence, it's only a matter of time before more protestors are killed."

The article closes with these poignant words:

> "Victims of 'justifiable homicides' in the United States are predominantly African American. The outcome of the verdict is going to lead to more vigilante killings by white shooters playing cops. Without the veil of legal repercussions and white vigilantes on the prowl at protests, the body count will only rise."[22]

Numerous people in the African American community, including attorneys, have pointed to the double standard of justice in American evidenced by the Rittenhouse case. One of them is Cornell William Brooks, former president and CEO of the NAACP and now a professor at Harvard University. Speaking in response to the Rittenhouse verdict, he said, "I don't have to tell you this, there is no set of circumstances, no reading of the law, no rendering of the imagination, in which a Black person could get away with this."[23]

Not to be outdone, race car driver, Bubba Wallace, who was born to a Black mother and a white father, tweeted moments after the Rittenhouse verdict, "Ha, let the boy be Black and it would've been life . . . hell he would've had his life taken before the bull**** trial.. sad."[24]

Perhaps the biggest display of white supremacy in America's recent past is the January 6, 2021, insurrection of the United States Capitol. Donald Trump was soundly defeated by Joe Biden in the 2020 election (306-232 electoral votes). Trump refused to concede and began propounding the Big Lie that the election was 'stolen' from him. Never mind that his own official responsible for election security, Chris Krebs, called the 2020 elections "the most secure in American history."[25] Also, Attorney General William Barr, Trump's hand-picked yes-man, said that there was no widespread voter fraud that could have changed the outcome of the election.[26]

Yet, even before the vote count was complete, Trump started attacking the integrity of the elections. Then, he and his supporters started publicizing plans to thwart the official certification of votes in the House of Representatives. On December 19, 2020, Trump drummed up support for a large rally on January 6, 2021, in Washington D.C. to coincide with the Congress' certification of Joe Biden's victory. "Be there, will be wild!" Trump tweeted.[27] With the help of social media, thousands of Trump supporters—predominantly white men—converged on Washington D.C. on January 6. In a pre-coup rally, Trump goaded his radical supporters to "walk down to the Capitol" and "take back our country." He also hinted that he would join them in the attack on the Capitol.

Then, the throng of white supremacists descended on the Capitol. Most wore MAGA hats. Many of the marchers came equipped with tactical gear. In the investigations following the riot, it turned out that many of the insurrections were current or former members of the military. Rioters took guns, pepper spray and zip ties (obviously with the intent of restraining captors). Some took Confederacy flags and used them as weapons.

The marchers broke down police barricades, pepper sprayed the Capitol police and attacked them viciously. Other rioters scaled the walls of the Capitol building. They broke through the doors, smashed windows, pummeled police officers and yelled "Where's Mike Pence." Their intent was to capture the Vice President and hang him on the noose that was erected outside the Capitol. The reason? Pence ignored Trump's repeated requests to call the election in his favor instead of carrying out his constitutional duty of certifying the elections. Rioters took over House Speaker Nancy Pelosi's office, and one rioter sat in the House Speaker's chair and put his boot on her desk. The message was clear: He is a white American, so this is his house. He is entitled!

The rioters beat police officers mercilessly. One officer screamed in agony as he was stuck in a doorway while rioters squeezed the heavy door like a vice against his body. Four protesters died as a result of the insurrection. Also, one Capitol police officer died on the scene and four others, who were severely beaten and/or traumatized, died by suicide. What's more, it took $1.5 million of our tax money to repair the Capitol building after the attack.[28]

While the January 6 insurrection was unfolding and in the aftermath of the attack, several members of the media, civil rights community as well as regular Americans pointed to the dichotomy between the law enforcement response of January 6 and the Black Lives Matter protests. Since December, Trump and his minions had been talking about a large 'Stop the Steal' rally at the Capitol on January 6. Also, Internet chatter leading up to the insurrection clearly indicated that a huge attack was imminent. In fact, intelligence analysts found "significant chatter" on several online sources. However, they neglected to report it because they considered the chatter to be "hyperbole."[29] This begs the question: Would the Department of Homeland Security ignore such chatter if it were between members of Black Lives Matter or a home-based Islamic group? I think not!

So, why didn't the authorities prepare for the throng of angry protestors? They knew Trump's supporters were irate over the ex-president's election loss and were hell-bent on seeing that Trump got a second term in office. I remember watching in horror as the angry mob took over the Capitol building. "Where's the police?" "Where's the National Guard?" I screamed at the TV screen.

Speaking to the 'white privilege in plain view' attack, Chidozie Obasi writes in *Harper's Bazaar*, "When the Black Lives Matter protests took place in June 2020 after George Floyd's murder, Black protesters faced tear gas, flash grenades and rubber bullets. Many sustained serious injuries."

Obasi also points out that in the midst of the January 6 melee, some protesters took selfies with law enforcement officers. The writer also notes that the different police response "exemplifies how much racial disparity is ingrained in the nation's system and how white privilege sits at the heart of racial injustice."

Then, Obasi states:

> "If Black people were the ones climbing up walls and causing havoc, the consequences would have been far more devastating. More guns would have been fired and the death toll would have been much higher, all at the hands of white power. To put it simply: if you are white and angry you get away with untold crimes, but if you are Black and show a sentiment of anxiety, if you protest for basic human rights, you are demonized."[30]

2. White privilege disproportionately values white people

Okay. Time for a true confession: I've been an advertising copywriter for most of my adult life. Most of the ads, brochures, commercials, ad campaigns and collateral materials I've written have been directed to white people. A key component of most of my promotional copy is reinforcing the value my audience members place on themselves. Because based on their status (monetary, lifestyle, professional, etc.) they 'deserve' the stuff I'm selling—such as fancy motorhomes, boats, appliances, solid hardwood furniture, insurance policies or mutual funds.

So, I admit it. Like other ad people, I leverage the disproportionate value white society places on itself in order to sell them more stuff! But, hey, it's the capitalistic way!

The disproportional value white people place on themselves has a sinister side: It undermines the value white people often place on people of color. Here are a few examples:

- White doctors and other medical providers routinely under-treat Black and Brown patients for pain as compared to white patients. This is based on the view that Black and Brown patients do not feel pain to the same degree as white patients.[31] Studies also show that Black and Brown women receive lower-quality preventive health care than white women.[32]

- While votes were still being counted during the 2020 elections, Donald Trump tried to invalidate the votes in cities like Philadelphia, Milwaukee and Atlanta. Trump was well aware that a vast majority of the voters in these cities were people of color. So, their vote was not as 'important' as those of the white people in the suburbs and rural areas of those states.

3. White privilege means society is structured around and for white people

America was founded by white people—many of whom self-identity as Christian—who held the view that they were entitled to all the riches this great land possessed. This view was the driving force behind Manifest Destiny—the idea that the United States is destined by God to expand its domination from sea to shining sea. Manifest Destiny did not include sharing property with America's indigenous settlers. Rather, it meant forcibly removing Native Americans from homes and lands they possessed for thousands of years. It meant confining Native Americans to reservations or exterminating them outright. Manifest Destiny also manifested itself in the effort among white Christians to 'Christianize' the Native Americans by forcing them to speak the English language, reject their own cultural practices and adopt European culture.[33]

White privilege means, then and now, that society is

structured around and for white people. This misplaced, disproportionate sense of value has been the primary motivation behind chattel slavery in the United States, segregation and the present-day white nationalist movement.

Stated differently, white privilege is white dominance.

Chapter 8
So What Exactly is Racism?

In 1964, the United States Supreme Court was adjudicating the case, Jacobellis v. Ohio, which involved determining the legal threshold for pornography. In the process of the deliberations, Justice Potter Stewart said, "I shall not today attempt further to define the kinds of material I understand to be embraced...But I know it when I see it ..."[1] The way the term *racism* is thrown around, one may think that defining racism is as nebulous as the Supreme Court defining pornography. But this is not the case. Racism is rather easy to define. However, the manifestations of racism are often subtle and indirect. But they're just as potent!

Racism is prejudice plus exclusion

Some antiracist proponents define racism as prejudice plus power. I concur with this definition as it relates to institutional racism. The Aspen Institute defines institutional racism as "policies and practices within and across institutions that, intentionally or not, produce outcomes that chronically favor, or put a racial group at a disadvantage."[2] As such, institutional racism is indirect and impersonal. And it manifests itself in discrimination against people of color in areas such as employment, housing, education, health care and criminal justice.

In practical terms, institutional racism may take the form of a property owners refusing to rent apartments to tenants based on their race or ethnicity. Or, it happens when country clubs refuse memberships to people of color. Institutional racism can also show up in the form of an organization refusing to hire candidates of color despite their qualifications and experience. (Racist organizations often claim that they don't discriminate.) Or, it could be financial institutions prohibiting people of color from obtaining loans based on where they live (a practice called 'redlining').

However, the prejudice plus power definition does not apply to acts of racial hostility between peers of different races, because neither exercises power over the other. For example, if a white person in an organization refuses to sit down for a cup of coffee with a Black person with the same standing in the organization, the white person would still be racist.

Or, if a white teenager fails to invite a Latino classmate to his or her house for a birthday party because of deep-seated resentment of people of color, that's racial discrimination. Here are four takeaways regarding racism:

1. Racism starts with prejudice

Of the many definitions I have found for racism, the one I have found the most accurate in all situations is one I concocted myself. Racism is prejudice plus exclusion. *Merriam Webster* defines prejudice as "an adverse opinion or leaning formed without just grounds or before sufficient knowledge."[3] In his book, *Dismantling Racism, The Continuing Challenge to White America*, Joseph Barndt defines prejudice as having "an opinion without knowing the facts, and to hold onto those opinions even after contrary facts are known."[4]

Everyone is prejudiced in one way or another. In antiracism seminars I have conducted, I asked attendees to share their prejudices. The answers were predictable and unpredictable, serious and funny. Attendees said they were prejudiced against spiders, cats and large dogs. One man said he is prejudiced against Islamic people. Then he quickly added, "Although I know I shouldn't be." One woman said with a smile that she is prejudiced against huge body builders. And another woman said she detests motorcycle riders. To which she added, "Although I know several pastors who ride bikes." Then, I shared my biggest prejudice. "I love just about everything about my home country of Jamaica," I would tell the class, "Except for the reptiles. I think they're gross!" (Like every other well-watered tropical country, Jamaica has an abundance of lizards, toads, frogs, snakes, crocodiles and other creepy crawlies.)

How does prejudice apply to racism? Race prejudice means having distorted opinions about other races. For example, I have heard racist stereotypes used against Italians, Mexicans, Asians (including Chinese, Korean and Indian people), Africans and, of course, African Americans. In fact, Trump frequently made such racist statements (as is detailed earlier in this book).

A friend of mine and her son were victims of race prejudice that left the little boy traumatized and the mother in tears. A professional and a woman of color, my friend had recently moved into a small Midwestern town. She took her six-year-old son, who I will call Bobby, to a white dentist for the first time. Little Bobby was a model child. He was quiet, well liked, well-behaved and a great student. As soon as the dentist saw Bobby, he freaked out. The dentist said he couldn't treat Bobby because he was sure the quiet little guy would be disruptive. My friend told the doctor that she was new in town and did not know any other dentist. The dentist was undeterred. By this time, Bobby was in tears, as was his mother. She concluded that the only reason the dentist refused to treat Bobby was because of his race.

2. Exclusion is a key element of racism

We've established that racism starts with holding a prejudicial attitude against someone of another race for no particular reason. Coupled with prejudice is a second major element: exclusion. In a sense, they come as a package—like peanut butter and jelly. Exclusion takes the form of white people refusing to develop normal personal relationships with people of color simply on the basis of their race, ethnicity or national origin. Examples are white people excluding people of color from being house guests, workout or golfing buddies. Or it might be refusing to share secrets and family photos. It's that simple. And that complicated!

Years ago, while living in a small Midwestern town, I served on a committee with an older African American man I'll call Mike. I learned that Mike had accomplished quite a lot in his lifetime. Mike told me that while serving in the US Army, he was scheduled to land on Normandy Beach on D-Day. But he missed the boat—literally. Instead, he landed in Cherbourg, about 60 miles west of Normandy three days after the bloody Normandy invasion. Upon returning home, Mike started working with the post office and worked his way up to being the town's first Black postmaster.

"The town fully accepted me as a Black man," Mike said assuredly. "No one ever treated me with disrespect," he continued.

I told Mike that I am happy he was so well received. Then

I asked, "Did any of the white people in the town invite you and your lovely wife to their home for Thanksgiving?"

"No," Mike replied.

"Did they invite you to go golfing with them?" I asked.

Mike shook his head.

"How about to a family cookout or church service?" I probed.

There was a furrow in Mike's brow. "Come to think of it, I was never included in the lives of any white people in town," Mike responded.

Racism means exclusion.

Another way to look at exclusion is to frame it as a matter of the heart. I mentioned earlier that I am prejudiced against reptiles. Last summer, my wife and I visited the zoo in our city—as we try to do several times each year. One exhibit we saw was that of an iguana. The large fella was perched in a picture-perfect manner on a tree limb. My wife, being the lover of just about every critter, started talking to the large reptile. She voiced admiration of the beautiful shades of green on his scaly body. She voiced admiration of his confident pose.

Then, she asked me to shoot a photo of him on my cell phone. I refused. Instead, I started to admire the furry mammals in the adjoining cage. While I was admiring the adventurous little foxes, I overheard snippets of my wife's conversation with the zoo attendant. Later, as we shared recollections of our time at the zoo, I repeated my disgust of the iguana and his distant cousins. "I loved all the animals," I said, "Except for the iguana and the gators."

My wife's eyes flashed with a gleam of revelation. "Honey, you need to set aside all your stereotypes about reptiles and give the iguana a chance. You need to evaluate him on his own merits."

Before I got a chance to enter an objection, my wife continued. "I kinda felt the same way as you do," she said, "but the zoo attendant changed my mind." My wife explained that the attendant told her that visiting Horace, the iguana, was the highpoint of each day.

"She told me he actually has a personality. You just gotta get to know him!" she smiled.

Then it dawned on me. My encounter with Horace was the quintessential picture of prejudice—any type of prejudice. For example, in an antiracist seminar, a man said he was prejudiced against people with tattoos. But his views changed when his daughter announced she got a tattoo on her lower back to commemorate her completion of a Ph.D.

My encounter with Horace also reminded me of the nature of race prejudice. Once people from one race lay aside their stereotypes, open their hearts and begin to accept people from other races on their own terms, healing can begin.

My response to Horace mirrors the nature of excluding others based on race. The problem is that people of color often do not know they are being excluded because of their race. They often assume that they are left out of conversations, relationships and the like due to other reasons, such as differences in lifestyle. The story of my relationship with Roger illustrates this point.

Years ago, my wife and I became well acquainted with a white couple about our age and who attended our church. I'll call the husband Roger and his wife Mary. Roger and Mary served as missionaries in South America, where they worked with indigenous people. They were fluent in Spanish. From everything I could tell, the couple was the most committed and exemplary followers of Jesus you could find.

I served on a church committee with Roger. During meetings, he always raised an objection to every point I made. Also, he always posed an opposing view to observations I made while teaching an adult Sunday school class or while making a contribution as a student. I assumed that Roger was just being his ornery self and forgot about the matter.

Then, I got a wake-up call when I attended a meeting of church leaders and missionaries in our denomination. After a moving sermon and a call to commitment, I remained seated with my eyes closed. Moments later, I heard heavy breathing beside me and felt an arm over my shoulders. I opened my eyes and looked to my right. It was Roger. His eyes were red, and tears streamed down his cheeks.

"I have resented you all these years because of your race," Roger said. "Will you forgive me?"

I was dumbfounded. It did not dawn on me that Roger was a racist. "I did not know you had those feelings," I said. "But, of course, I forgive you," I replied.

We hugged, and became the best of friends from that point on.

3. Most racial acts are subtle rather than overt

When I was a teenager in Jamaica, I saw on the evening news the disgraceful footage of white people spraying Black demonstrators with fire hoses in the American South. I saw photos of white people assaulting African Americans. I saw clips of Dr. Martin Luther King calling for racial equality. And it made no sense to me. So, I made two false assumptions: First, I assumed that only 'bad' people (people who did not have a personal relationship with Jesus Christ) were racists. And second, I assumed that racism only involved overt and blatant acts—such as cross burnings on the lawn of a person of color, calling people of color nigger, blocking people of color from bathrooms and so forth.

After immigrating to the United States, I faced racial discrimination for the first time. And I discovered that people who call Jesus their Savior and Lord can be—and oftentimes, are—racist. I also discovered that racism is most often subtle rather than overt.

Let me illustrate. Before the digital era, I served as a photographer and staff writer at a mission organization that sent missionaries from the United States to Latin America, Africa and Europe. I was the organization's main news writer, promotional writer and photographer. I served as associate editor and contributing writer for the organization's flagship publication plus as editor for a number of other periodicals.

I took the position at the mission agency as what I believed to be the call of God on my life—a call that motivated me to study theology at a Bible college in Jamaica. So, I closed my small advertising agency in order to fulfill this call. After more than three years in the mission agency, an opening developed for a director, since the current director retired. The mission agency tapped a number of people within the organization for the position. They all turned down the offer.

Finally, I officially applied for the position. Within days of my application, the president of the organization orchestrated a campaign to fire me. He circulated lies and innuendos about my job performance and conduct—despite the fact that I received stellar evaluations and pay raises each year.

Then the president called in a psychologist to formulate a paper trail on which to fire me. The psychologist conducted a series of meetings with the department in which members took turns accusing me of all manner of issues. They questioned my judgment regarding my editorial decisions. Other members of the department were assertive in their respective roles, and no one questioned them about it. But I dare not be assertive, although my job called for me to take initiative!

Finally, one member after another confessed to the group that they resented me because of my race. After several months of these turbulent weekly meetings, we reached a point of total harmony. Whew!

The psychologist then told the president that all 'conflicts' in the department were laid to rest. (I'm always fascinated by how people of color get blamed for other people's racism.)

That night, I went home with the feeling that a large burden was lifted from my shoulders. My colleagues finally confessed their racism. I forgave them. So, all is good. Right?

Wrong! The psychologist did not give the racist mission board president the result he wanted. So, on the following day, I received a lengthy 'work plan' that essentially gave me, a manager, one area of autonomy: going to the bathroom. Every other duty called for someone to shadow me. Things got so ridiculous, that the outgoing director accompanied me into the darkroom. I chuckled as he had to stay with me in the absolute darkness as I loaded films onto spools and dropped them in the developing tank canister. Also, when I printed pictures and kept a red 'safe light' on for illumination, I sarcastically asked the outgoing director to tell me when he thought the photos were developed enough to be moved to the stop bath. (He knew nothing about darkroom work.)

On an eventful morning a few weeks later, the president fired me before a full meeting of staff at the mission agency, plus at least two other church agencies. (A tearful friend of mine told me the story.) Then, the outgoing director accompanied me as I cleared out my personal items and moved them into my car.

And I was fired with no severance payment *two weeks before Christmas*!

At no time during the entire process did anyone call me Black, nigger or any derogatory term. Neither did anyone place such terms or statements in writing. I presented my unjust firing to the board that oversees the mission agency. As I looked around the room, I took note of the people who were going to decide my fate. The board members were essentially the bosses of the mission board president. In the crowd was my doctor, a church planter I interviewed for articles on several occasions, a businesswoman I knew and respected and a Black pastor who I thought was a friend.

I closed my presentation by asking the mission board president to participate in a foot-washing ceremony with me. Following the example of Jesus, believers throughout the centuries have been washing each other's feet as a sign of mutual submission. Everyone in the room knew exactly what it meant. The board president did not budge. And the governing board unanimously upheld the decision of the president to fire me.

In an attempt to keep my record clear for future employment and to receive some severance money, I took the matter to the Equal Employment Opportunity Commission (EEOC) in my state. In the process, I retained an attorney who specialized in discrimination law. I handed over boxes of documents supporting my case. But I apologized that I did not have a 'smoking gun'—verbally or in writing.

"Those would be nice to have," my attorney said, "But most often, I do not get such evidence." Then the attorney explained that in America, racism often boils down to being treated differently. And in my case, different treatment abounded. I was the only full-time employee in the headquarters office who was non-white. I was eminently qualified for the position. I had Bible school training plus college training in photography, marketing and advertising. Also, I had run a successful ad agency, in which I placed ads for international companies in nationwide magazines and newspapers and on local radio and TV stations. No one in the history of the mission agency was this qualified in mass media. And no one had been terminated like I was!

In an arbitration session, the mission agency agreed to purge my record of anything negative, give me a natural job reference and give me three months' severance payment.

And this all happened because they treated me differently than they do white people. The organization's racism was always subtle rather than overt!

4. Antiracism means equality—plain and simple

Being an antiracist person has nothing to do with how much you help people of color. It has nothing to do with whether you host people of color as house guests. Also, being antiracist has nothing to do with how much your congregation or denomination gives to help people of color in the United States or overseas. Being antiracist is all about treating people of color as equal—not better, not worse—equal!

My interaction with a white woman who had severe disabilities illustrates what it means to be an antiracist person. Years ago, my wife and I occasionally invited Donna, a white woman with disabilities, for dinner on a Friday or Saturday night. On one occasion, Donna asked to be picked up from a women's shelter where she volunteered. My instructions were to pick up Donna at 6 p.m. So, I parked outside the shelter and knocked on the door. After a few minutes, the door opened a few inches. I noticed the chain strung across the door and a pair of blue eyes staring at me. The door closed suddenly. Then, a few minutes later, the door opened once again, and the same blue eyes stared at me behind the chained-up door.

After what seemed like an hour (although it may have only been five minutes) the door opened and Donna emerged, a crutch in each hand and a broad smile on her face. During the drive back to my house, Donna filled me in on the reason for the delay. Naturally, she repeated the story, with even more drama, over dinner.

"I told my supervisor that my friend will be picking me up," Donna said. She added that the supervisor asked what the person who would be picking her up looked like. "Oh, he's a guy—about 6 feet tall, medium build, black hair and green eyes."

There was an impish grin on Donna's face as she continued her story. "Then, my supervisor said, 'You didn't tell me he is Black.'"

"It didn't cross my mind," Donna grinned.

This is what it means to be an antiracist!

Part 3

It's Time to Rethink White Nationalism

If my people, who are called by my name, will humble themselves and pray and seek my face and turn from their wicked ways, then I will hear from heaven, and I will forgive their sin and will heal their land.

II Chronicles 7:14 (NIV)

Chapter 9

Is America Specifically Ordained by God?

I once heard the story about a large bird of prey that was seen feasting on a dead animal in the midst of a fast-moving river. The bird was so focused on its dinner that its large, sharp claws became entangled in the carcass. Of course, the bird's wings weren't strong enough to lift itself and the carcass. As the carcass with the attached bird kept moving downstream, the bird realized it was getting precariously close to a waterfall. So, the bird needed to extricate itself from the carcass and fly off to safety or remain entangled and plunge into the abyss.

The white evangelical Church in America is facing such a dilemma. The Church has aligned itself so deeply with the lies, racism, mean-spiritedness and corruption of the

Trumpian wing of the Republican party, that its only hope lies in extricating itself from the ungodly alliance. But the Church must act fast! First, the Church needs to pursue the mission of calling people to faith in Christ—being agents of reconciliation rather than agents of a political movement. Second, the Church should adopt a 'colony of heaven' lifestyle in which Christians follow Christ so closely that the world sees them as citizens of heaven here on earth.

Before discussing the rightful role the Church should play in politics and society at large, we need to lay some groundwork regarding prevailing views about the place of God in the life of America. Stated differently, the Church's adherence to Christian nationalism is a major stumbling block to the Church assuming its rightful place here on earth.

The United States of America is a great nation. We were founded just over 200 years ago. Yet, we're the most powerful nation on the planet. We have the world's largest economy and by far the largest military budget.[1] Also, the US represents one of the largest democracies on earth. (India beats us for the top slot.) And with the rise of Trumpism, our democracy is now considered to be 'flawed.'[2] Also, as church leaders like to point out, we field more missionaries overseas[3] and contribute more money for missionary work beyond our borders than any other country.

So, does this mean we are specially ordained by God? Many Christians believe this. Some refer to the core concept of John O'Sullivan's 1845 essay in which he presents his belief in Manifest Destiny. This is the view that God gave the

United States the special mission of conquering the continent from sea to shining sea in the name of democracy.[4] Indeed, the notion of American expansionism based on our supposed special divine status has been the impetus behind our participation in two world wars and other military conquests. It has also been a driving force behind the way we conduct missionary pursuits. Because along with our desire to take the message of redemption through the sacrifice of Christ on the cross, we see the need to export our culture as well. This includes everything from baseball to burgers, worship style to wardrobe.

Some Christians even go as far as to say that our nation is God's 'new Israel' in the sense that we live in a 'Christian' nation that exhibits God-like characteristics in or laws, system of government and freedom of religion. And as ancient Israel reflected the attributes of Jehovah in its government structure, national religion, laws and culture, so should we as a nation.

The rise of Christian nationalism

The emergence of Trumpian hyper-Americanism and Trump's pandering to white evangelicals to get their vote has given rise to a new extremist view among some branches of the evangelical faith. That's Christian nationalism. As Amanda Tyler, Executive Director, Baptist Joint Commission for Religious Liberty observes, "We've seen the rise of Christian nationalism at different periods in our history, including in the 1950s, around the Cold War, where we saw increased evidence of government speech, such as 'In God We Trust' (on our coins and) adding 'under God' to the Pledge of Allegiance.[5]

Speaking to a group of evangelicals, Trump said, "We are Americans, and Americans kneel to God and God alone."[6] Predictably, the audience broke out in thunderous applause. The statement, of course, is patently false. The Constitution of the United States grants religious plurality. And Americans bow to numerous gods on a daily basis.

Paul D. Miller, professor at Georgetown University, defines Christian nationalism as "the belief that the American nation is defined by Christianity, and that the government should take active steps to keep it that way."[7] And Amanda Tyler observes, "Christian nationalism is a political ideology and a cultural framework that tries to merge our identities as Americans and Christians."[8]

In one of his *Reality Check* editions, CNN's John Avlon notes that Christian nationalism has grown from "a system advocated by a few folks on the far right to an increasingly prominent article of political faith inside the Republican party." To that point, far-right extremists like Marjorie Taylor Green, GOP representative from Georgia's 14th district, proudly proclaim themselves as Christian nationalists.[9]

On the surface, the goals of Christian nationalism seem noble. Which follower of Jesus can argue with aims like reducing abortion, reinstating prayer in schools and increasing positive references to God in the public space?

But look below the surface, and you'll find that Christian

nationalism is largely unchristian and racist. Four falsehoods lie at the core of Christian nationalism:

Error No. 1: America is a Christian nation that's divinely appointed by God

This view supports the Christian nationalists' belief that America should develop a strong Christian culture. Along with this view comes the notion that Christians should have an elevated position in the public square because they are heirs of the true or essential heritage of American culture. So, in effect, Christians have the right to define what it means to be American.

Some Christian nationalists believe the Constitution should be amended to recognize America's Christian heritage. Others want the sanitized, Christian nationalist's take on American history to become incorporated into school curricula. Yet others aspire to see clampdowns on immigration to keep America whiter. This would mean restricting immigration from Black and Brown countries. And, of course, Christian nationalists hold that government should legislate morality—hence efforts to ban abortion, even if it means allowing no exemptions for rape or incest. Also, some extremists would say it should be a crime for doctors and other health care providers to abort a fetus that's not viable or is putting the life of the mother in jeopardy.

Is mandating 'righteous' behavior a good idea? Many evangelical theologians believe it is not a good idea.

Constantine R. Campbell, a professor and associate research director at Sydney (Australia) College of Divinity observes:

> "When Christians say that America is God's country or that we are called to turn America into Christ's kingdom, we betray (that we have) a serious misunderstanding of the Bible. Jesus has not given his followers a mandate to turn earthy political kingdoms into the kingdom of Christ. Do we really think we can establish Jesus' kingdom through meager political activism when Jesus died and rose again to bring his kingdom?"

Campbell further argues that the Church should not believe that it can turn America's worldly culture into the kingdom of God. Not only is that impossible but it disrespects Jesus' teaching and His mission."[10]

Is America divinely appointed by God in a way that can't be said of every other nation? Certainly, much of the success of the United States arises from its natural resources and America's stewardship of those resources. Also, our educational acumen and strong work ethic go a far way in making us a prosperous nation. But every objective thinker would have to conclude that much of our 'greatness' has occurred through the exploitation of people of color, as exemplified by slavery and our appropriating natural resources from Native Americans. Does exploitation of others grant us favored status with God?

Many people who are steeped in Judeo-Christian beliefs

disagree with the view that America is divinely appointed by God. Let's review the circumstances around God's special relationship with Israel and see if we can extrapolate whether a similar or parallel relationship exists with the United States.

Genesis 12 records that God appeared to an idol worshipper named Abram and informed him that he would become the 'father' of the nation of Israel. Abraham (God changed his name) obeyed God, left what is present-day Southern Iraq and journeyed to Israel. God promised to create a great nation from Abraham's descendants. God also said Abraham would become famous. Then, God said He would bless all the people on planet earth through Abraham (Genesis 12:1-3).

This phrase—that all people will be blessed through Abraham's descendants—is a direct reference to Jesus, who came to earth as a descendant of Abraham. Through Jesus' death and resurrection, God opened the way for everyone on earth who believes in Him to receive forgiveness from sin and eternal life.

Hundreds of years after God made the promise to Abraham, God established the children of Israel as a theocracy in the land of Palestine. Prior to entering the land, God told the people, who had just been miraculously delivered from bondage in Egypt, that God chose them for a two-fold reason. First, God said Israel was chosen because God made a pledge to Israel's ancestors (Abraham). "The Lord loved you and kept the oath he swore to your ancestors," (Deuteronomy 7:8 NIV).

Second, God said he chose Israel so they would be a showcase of holy living. "For you are a people holy to the Lord your God," (Deuteronomy 7:6 NIV).

To help Israel become a holy nation, God instructed them to destroy all 'pagan' gods in the land, refrain from intermarriage with people who do not worship the God of Abraham and follow the laws God gave the people. In essence, God wanted Israel to be a showcase—an 'Exhibit A'—of righteousness, holiness and justice. As a survey of the historic books in the Old Testament reveals, God blessed Israel when they obeyed his laws and lived holy lives. And God judged them when they didn't.

So, Israel is unique! To equate the United States, or any other nation for that matter, with this aspect of Israel's identity is capricious and absurd. In fact, other nations at the cusp of greatness also assumed that they were divinely appointed by God. Great Britain, Spain and France claimed divine appointments when they authorized and financed exploration of the New World. Because their mission was supposedly to convert the natives to Christianity.[11] To this point, John H. Redekop says in *Politics Under God:*

> "An especially difficult problem arises when a country is tempted to think of itself as God's favorite, even as a new Israel. While it may happen, as in Old Testament times, that God decides to use one country to punish another country for its evil ways, it is inappropriate for any government or country to describe itself as God's

agent. Such a selection of decision is strictly God's prerogative. In our day, so-called Christian-Americanism has been a temptation for some American Christians. In earlier times, similar cultic claims gained support in Russia, Great Britain, Spain, Germany and other lands.[12]

And professor and author Miguel A. De La Torre explains, "Let's be clear: no political party, especially the Republican or the Democratic, is ordained by God. No president, emperor, prime minister, king or queen is ever or ever was ordained by God."[13]

Here's the bottom line: If we hold the view that America is specially chosen by God due to its might and privilege, we would also have to believe that God somehow approved of the acts that made America 'great' in the first place. I find this view at odds with my understanding of Scripture.

The idea that America is a Christian nation that's divinely appointed by God relates to the second misguided view of Christian nationalists.

Error No. 2: America's founders wanted to create a nation based on Christian principles. So, they had no intention of founding a religiously-pluralistic country.

There is no doubt that many of our Founding Fathers were men of deep faith. (There were no 'Founding Mothers.') Many of these founders made famous statements regarding their faith in God and in God's role in the creation of America. Founder Father Patrick Henry said:

> "It cannot be emphasized too strongly or too often that this great nation was founded, not by religionists, but by Christians; not on religions, but on the gospel of Jesus Christ. For this very reason peoples of other faiths have been afforded asylum, prosperity, and freedom of worship here."[14]

Despite Patrick Henry's bold assertion, the Founding Fathers deliberately structured the United States as a religiously neutral nation. The First Amendment to the Constitution states: "Congress shall make no law respecting an establishment of religion, or prohibiting the free exercise thereof . . ."[15]

Any notion that the United States is a 'Christian' nation was laid to rest in 1797—a mere 21 years after the Declaration of Independence. US ships had begun sailing under the US flag. So, they were not covered by treaties as they had been when they sailed under the British flag. As a result, in 1797, the US Congress ratified the Treaty of Tripoli (now Libya) in an attempt to prevent the so-called Barbary pirates from attacking US ships. The Libyan pirates were Muslim. The treaty made it clear that the United States was not a 'Christian' nation, and as such, America was not intrinsically hostile to Muslims. Article 11 of the treaty says in part, "The Government of the United States of America is not, in any sense, founded on the Christian religion..."[16]

Christian nationalists generally hold the view that Christianity should be given a privileged status in society. This is based on the premise that America is a 'Christian' country. Or, as Paul D. Miller puts it: "Christian nationalism . . . accurately describes American nationalists who believe American identity is inextricable from Christianity."[17] This is why so many Christians support the placement of religious icons like the 10 Commandments and Christmas nativity scenes on public property. It also supports the idea that at Christmastime, the normative greeting of Christians and non-Christians alike should be "Merry Christmas" instead of "Happy Holidays." In fact, Trump, in his repeated campaign of bamboozling white evangelicals that he cares about Christianity, waged a campaign to replace the greeting, "Happy Holidays" with "Merry Christmas."[18]

As many scholars point out, the quest among white Christians to 'keep America Christian' is more about maintaining a white Christian culture rather than retaining the foundational elements of the Christian faith per se. In other words, it's more about the potluck dinners, small group get-togethers, golf outings, worship style and political activism than the content of sermons. And these practices fall overwhelmingly within the domain of white Christians.

Paradoxically enough, to the extent that the United States is currently 'Christian,' it is getting less so. A growing number of Christian leaders are coming to terms with the reality that America is increasingly becoming more non-Christian. Pew Research Center estimates that in 2020, about 64 percent of Americans self-identified as Christians. However, the Center states that if present trends continue, "Christians could make up less than half of the U.S. population within a few decades."[19]

Another trend in American culture is exacerbating the angst faced by the white evangelical church: the decreasing white majority in American society. The Brookings Institute projects that "the United States will become a 'minority white' nation by 2045."[20] This means that for the first time in its history, the United States will have more people of color than white people. This may well be increasing the impetus among the Christian right to shore up the Christian nationalist agenda more than ever.

Like many other evangelical Christians, I would love to see multitudes of Americans become converted to Christianity. But that's not to say that I am revolted by people in America practicing numerous non-Christian religions—or having no affinity to any particular deity. However, Christian nationalists do not share my view on this matter. For them, 'true' Americans embrace Christianity—even it means a Trump-like lip service to the faith with no corresponding belief system or lifestyle habits.

To this point, Georgetown professor Paul D. Miller notes that white nationalists construct their nation by defining who is and who is not part of that nation. He observes, "Christian nationalism tends to treat other Americans as second-class citizens." He also points out that Christian nationalists do not respect the full religious liberty of all Americans.[21]

Indeed, the white supremacist elements of Christian nationalism are clearly reflected in the third element of Christian nationalism.

Error No. 3: America should be led by white men, and all Black and Brown people should accept this reality

The disgust white evangelicals showed for Barack Obama and the admiration they showed for Donald Trump is a clear indication of the Christian nationalists view that white men should lead and Black men (and women) should stay out of the way. No one presents this dichotomy better than John Pavlovitz, Christian pastor and author. In one of his brilliantly written blogs, Pavlovitz says:

> "For eight years they (white evangelicals) watched you relentlessly demonize a Black president—a man faithfully married for 26 years, a doting father and husband without a hint of moral scandal or the slightest whiff of infidelity.
>
> They watched you deny his personal faith convictions, argue his birthplace and assail his character—all without cause or evidence. They saw you brandish Scriptures to malign him and use the laziest of racial stereotypes in criticizing him.
>
> And through it all, white evangelicals, you never once suggested that God placed him where he was. You never publicly offered prayers for him and his family.

You never welcomed him to your Christian universities. You never gave him the benefit of the doubt in any instance. You never spoke of offering him forgiveness or mercy.

Your evangelists never publicly thanked God for his leadership. Your pastors never took to the pulpit to offer solidarity with him. You never made any effort to affirm his humanity or show the love of Jesus to him in any quantifiable measure.

You violently opposed him at every single turn—without offering a single ounce of the grace you claim as the heart of your faith tradition. You jettisoned Jesus as you dispensed damnation on him.

And yet you give carte blanche to a white Republican man so riddled with depravity, so littered with extramarital affairs, so unapologetically vile, with such a vast resume of moral filth, that the mind boggles.

And the change in you is unmistakable. It has been an astonishing conversion to behold: a being born again.

With him, you suddenly find religion. With him, you're now willing to offer full absolution. With him, all is forgiven without repentance or admission. With him, you're suddenly able to see some invisible, deeply buried heart. With him, sin has become unimportant and compassion no longer a requirement. With him, you see only Providence."[22]

For Christian nationalists, the only legitimate leader—at any level of society—is a white man. Women of any race and people of color need not apply. And because white males are God's appointed leaders, people of color (and women) should voluntarily subject themselves to white leadership. Yet, the fourth guiding principle of Christian nationalists is understandable given the other three positions.

Error No 4: There is no separation between Church and state

In the Christian nationalists' view of America, the Church should enjoy a preferred status—one above all other religions or faith communities. In fact, U.S. Representative Lauren Boebert (R. Colo.) told a crowd of Colorado churchgoers, "The Church is supposed to direct the government. The government is not supposed to direct the Church . . . And I'm tired of this separation of Church and state junk."[23]

However, as every American learned as early as middle school, the Constitution of the United States spells out the doctrine that Church and state are separate: "Congress shall make no law respecting an establishment of religion, or prohibiting the free exercise thereof."[24]

To understand the separation of Church and state, we need to consider the factors that were in the minds of the Founders. These men knew about the turmoil and violence that took place in Europe because of religion. Rulers and members of the clergy had jostled for power or united to impose religious beliefs on the populace. The framers of the Constitution did not want that pattern of abuse to take place in the United States. As a result, the founders made no reference to God or the Bible in the Constitution. They deliberately separated Church from state.

To this point, George L. Alexander—a retired psychiatrist who has written widely for the Society of Friends (Quakers)—observes that the Constitution offers "the unique concept of deliberately separating Church and state. Some scholars view this as perhaps our greatest contribution to human history."[25]

Oddly enough, the separation of Church and state mandate keeps both the Church and the state within their respective guardrails. It means the Church cannot impose its will on all Americans, including Americans of non-Christian faiths or no faith at all. The National Day of Prayer provides a great example. In 1952, during the Korean War, the United States Congress designated a day for prayer. Then, in 1988, the law was amended to designate the first Thursday of May each year as the 'National Day of Prayer.'

I believe in the power of prayer and that the National Day of Prayer is a great idea. However, if the Church called the shots over the state, as some Christian nationalists desire, the Church could, for example, demand that everyone prays on the first Thursday of each May. Is this a good idea? At the very least, it would stir up widespread condemnation from non-Christians (and perhaps from Christians as well) about having religion forced down people's throats.[26]

As Paul D. Miller points out, "Empowering the state through 'morals legislation' to regulate conduct always carries the risk of overreaching, setting a bad precedent, and creating governing powers that could be used later against Christians."[27]

The Bible teaches, and history illustrates, that coercion is antithetical to the Christian faith. Belief has always been the entrance portal into the Faith. The Apostle Paul said, "Abraham believed God, and it was credited to him as righteousness," (Romans 4:3 NIV). And John 3:16, perhaps the most quoted verse in the Bible, states "whoever believes" in Jesus will receive everlasting life. Also, Colossians 2:6 reminds us, "So then, just as you received Christ Jesus as Lord (by faith), continue to live your lives in him," (NIV).

How smart is the idea of merging Church and state in present-day America? Let's look at the genesis of the Church-state merger: Emperor Constantine in fourth-century Rome. Constantine ruled over the Roman Empire from about A.D. 306-337. At that time, the Church had been in existence for less than 300 years. The Church had earlier suffered extreme persecution and was considered a fringe group among a host of religions in the ancient world.

But things changed when Constantine was leading his army into a battle against a superior force in Italy. The emperor saw a vision of a cross and the phrase, "In this sign conquer." Constantine told the vision to his army and commanded his troops to place a sign representing the 'Highest God' on their shields. The emperor and his army won the battle, and Constantine vowed to follow God.[28]

What Constantine did next changed Christianity forever—for better *and* for worse. He essentially rolled the Church and the state into one. To his credit, Constantine took several actions that benefited the Church. Among them, he:

- Issued and edict granting freedom of worship;
- Ordered the restitution of property confiscated from Christians during their previous persecution;
- Legislated against gladiatorial combats;
- Made edicts on behalf of widows and orphans as well as the poor;
- Ruled against immorality, prostitution and injustices such as infanticide and the selling of children into slavery;
- Funded the construction of new church buildings.

As a result, Christians enjoyed freedom and privileges like never before. However, Constantine's Church-state merger negatively affected the Church in ways that reverberate to this day. Here are a few of these actions and their consequences:

- Due to the newly found popularity of Christianity, many joined the Church to gain favor with the emperor. Many 'converts' did not fully embrace the teachings of the Church. Rather, they clung to their pagan practices and incorporated them into the newly popular Christian movement. Paganism and secularism entered the Church.

- Over the ensuing centuries, the Church incorporated practices like the veneration of saints and angels, the use of statues and icons in worship and an unbiblical reverence for the Virgin Mary.

- Constantine gave bishops judicial and legal authority. This led to corruption among some leaders which resulted in the decline of spirituality among leaders and church members alike.

- Constantine tortured pagan priests to death, evicted non-Christians from their hometown and ordered the execution of magicians and soothsayers, among other atrocities.[29]

- Constantine made the decision to move the capital city of his empire from Rome to Byzantium, which lies at the entrance of the Black Sea. Over time, a rift developed between the Western Church in Rome and the Eastern Church in Byzantium, which was renamed Constantinople (present-day Istanbul). The Eastern Church later split from the Western Church, creating the Orthodox Church and the Roman Catholic Church respectively.[30]

- The Constantine-inspired Church-state model has since been replicated by numerous governments, resulting in the most atrocious acts, including

Church-sponsored slavery in the Americas and forced conversions in Mexico by the Conquistadors.

So, to everyone who would like to see an end to the Church-state divide in America, be careful what you wish for.

How 'Christian' is Christian nationalism? Paul D. Miller observes that Christian nationalism takes "the name of Christ as a fig leaf to cover its political program, treating the message of Jesus as a tool of political propaganda and the Church as the handmaiden and cheerleader of the state."[31] And Amanda Tyler puts it more bluntly. She says, "Christian nationalism is not Christianity."[32]

Chapter 10

How Should Christians Involve Themselves in Politics?

Evangelical Christianity in America fits hand in glove with politics. In an effort to be the 'salt of the earth' and the 'light of the world' in obedience to the words of Jesus, evangelicals like to see Christian principles reflected not just in their own lives but in the society as well. The political process provides unique opportunities to make this happen. As a result, Christians have thrown their weight behind causes like the abolition of slavery, Prohibition, civil rights legislation and pro-life legislation, just to name a few causes.

Indeed, many scholars and politicians point out the inevitability of Christian involvement in the political process. Redekop observes, "It is a myth to think that we can escape politics."[1] He also says:

"Most of us are greatly affected by political matters and are much more involved in politics than we may realize. Even the attempts to avoid political involvement do not eliminate people's political significance. Ultimately, the issue is not whether to be involved politically but how to be involved politically."[2]

Also, President Reagan said, "Religion and politics are necessarily related.[3]

So, the question is not whether most Christians will get involved in politics, but what level of involvement they will have?

I believe Christians can in good faith support the traditional positions of the Republican and Democratic parties all the way up to vying for political office themselves. (By 'traditional positions' for Republicans, I'm referring to lower taxes, free market capitalism, deregulation of corporations, and restrictions on labor unions, low government interference in the business sector and support of the private sector. Traditional Democratic beliefs include a strong government to regulate business, workers' rights, protection of the environment, equal pay for men and women as well as standing up for the middle class.)

Doesn't this mean that Christians will be supporting flawed candidates? Of course! Let's consider our recent presidents. In recent history, for example, Republicans sing the praises of Ronald Reagan, George H. W. Bush and George W. Bush. Meanwhile, Christians who lean Democratic heap accolades on Jimmy Carter, Bill Clinton, Barack Obama and Joe Biden.

All these presidents to a lesser or greater degree represented their respective Republican or Democratic positions. But their flaws as persons, or the positions they took on issues, have been widely criticized. Carter drew criticism for his weak foreign policy, epitomized by the failed rescue of hostages in Iran. Reagan received pushback for initiating mass incarcerations primarily of young Black and Brown men (and kick-starting the private prison industry) through legislation aimed at users of crack cocaine, the drug of choice for people of color. George H. W. Bush was blamed for leaving behind a spike in oil prices, due in part to the aftereffects of Iraq's invasion of Kuwait, the rise in unemployment and a dip in business and consumer confidence.[4] Despite all his legislative and foreign policy achievements, Bill Clinton will always be remembered for the Monica Lewinsky affair. George W. Bush received criticism for plunging the United States into war with Iraq and for his late and lack-luster response to Hurricane Katrina. And pundits criticized Barack Obama for failing to move aggressively on filling judicial nominations and for mishandling the rollout of the Affordable Care Act (Obamacare).

But the failures of all our past presidents combined fall far short of the horrific words and actions of Donald Trump. Yet, the morally depraved, ethically destitute, intellectually challenged, spiritually bankrupt, twice impeached, four times indicted ex-president remains the messiah of millions of white evangelicals. Unlike former presidents who gracefully bowed out of public life and immersed themselves into writing their memoirs or becoming involved in charitable causes, Trump has established himself as the de facto leader of the Republican party. He publicly backs GOP candidates who kiss up to him and support the Big Lie that the 2020 election was stolen. He continues to publicly castigate his political foes and lambaste federal institutions like the Justice Department and the FBI.

This begs the question: Are there any limits to when and how Christians should become involved in politics? Can Christians support any candidate? If so, what might be some guardrails?

The Christian ethic is at odds with party politics

Before we attempt to answer how Christians might get involved in politics and remain consistent with the teaching of Scripture, we need to explore a related matter: The Christian ethic is at odds with party practice and ideology. So, even in the best of circumstances, actively participating in the political process places ethical and spiritual hurdles that Christians must overcome.

Years ago, I ran my own advertising agency. In the quest for new clients and experiences, I accepted an invitation to promote a candidate who was running for state senate. As an ad guy, I am energized by competition. It's what drives me to write killer copy and create out-of-the-box ad campaigns.

But writing for a political candidate took me far out of my comfort zone.

For starters, I was expected to deliberately misstate the competing candidate's positions. For example, my client's competitor for office voted for an omnibus bill that included a potentially negative provision (as I understand often happens with such bills). I was asked to write a release that focused only on the negative component of the bill (representing a sliver of the budget) and totally ignore the bill's main—and positive—provision. I was expected to say something like, "All Joe Schmo stands for is wasting money on . . ." Another line I was given to flesh out ran something like this, "Joe Schmo is in league with the major oil companies and is against the little guys . . ."

Never in my long career as an ad copywriter was I ever expected to misconstrue facts or deliberately lie. Yes, on a daily basis, I present features and benefits of products and services in the most positive light. Yes, I establish products' 'Unique Sales Position'—what a particular product/service does, or is perceived to do, for the user better than any other product/service on the planet for the cost. But writing lies? Never.

Another big 'no-no' I faced was that I was expected to disseminate rumors about the competing candidate's personal life—including that of his wife. I considered this off limits. I recalled some of the other ad agencies in my city. We repeatedly pitched against each other for accounts. We stole each other's talent (art directors, account managers etc.) from time to time. But we never attacked each other personally—or for that matter attacked their next of kin.

I quit working for the candidate, wished him well, and never pursued working for a political candidate since. It seems to me that active involvement in party politics—anything beyond voting for candidates on election day—has some major challenges for Christians.

The first challenge is that politics is intrinsically divisive. In our strong two-party system, campaigning for political office and, if you win, drafting legislation as an elected official call for pitting your party against the other party. In practice, this often means lining up behind your party's position. As such, it involves glossing over unwise or negative views and ideas of your party and ignoring positive ideas put forward by the opposing party. I often chuckle when I hear candidates for office in my state talk about going to Washington to "shake things up." When they win, they inevitably go along with most positions—including stupid and mean-spirited ones—from their party leadership.

The involvement of the Christian Right in politics illustrates this ethical dilemma. Speaking to this matter, political scientists Kenneth D. Wald and Allison Calhoun-Brown observe:

> "Some thoughtful critics have wondered whether participation in politics, as inherently messy business, may compromise the integrity of people who get involved

precisely to secure higher levels of public integrity. Because evangelicals put such high stock in personal morality (as they understand it), they may be less willing to remain politically responsive to leaders who are compromised."[5]

In unmasking the quest of evangelical Christians to 'win' at all costs through the electoral process, Andy Stanley, founder of the Atlanta-based North Point Ministries, notes: "We rebrand slander as truth-telling."[6]

A second reason for believing that Christianity and deep involvement in party politics don't mix is that Christians should commit themselves to evangelism and discipleship instead of winning 'earthy' battles. The deep involvement of millions of Christians in the 2020 elections is a case in point.

In this regard, Campbell says, "Instead of pursuing cultural and political transformation of a nation, Christians ought to prioritize several other goals instead."[7]

Pastor Andy Stanley describes his big 'sin'—from many of his parishioners' viewpoint—over the 2020 election cycle. He refused to publicly endorse Donald Trump. Fact is, Stanley did not endorse Joe Biden either. He simply remained quiet regarding political matters. However, many churchgoers saw Stanley's actions as being uninformed at best and worthy of hellfire at worst. This led Stanley to write the book, *Not in it to Win it*.

Stanley says he did not want to write the book, but that

the division in the Church caused by the "recent political and cultural mayhem to distract us from what our Savior commanded us to do" motivated him to write the book.[8] The pastor continues, "When winning (an election) replaces following (Jesus) we are no longer following. We are no longer Christian as defined by the folks who originally coined the term."[9] He continues, "When a local church becomes preoccupied with saving America at the expense of saving Americans, it has forsaken its mission."[10] Stanley cautions that we dare not attempt to "save America" at the expense of "loving the American next door."[11]

A third stumbling block in the way of Christians—especially church leaders—getting involved in party politics is that publicly siding with a political party makes it difficult to be a faithful witness to people in the opposing party. To this point, Stanley points out that Christians or church leaders "who publicly align with a political party . . . relinquished their ability to make disciples of half their own nation, much less all nations."[12] He adds "In their attempt to save America from the other political party, they lost their opportunity to save half of America from their sin."[13]

A fourth reason active involvement in party politics is laden with challenges for Christians is that Americans are skeptical about the participation of Christians in politics. As Wald and Calhoun-Brown observe, "Americans are not very enthusiastic about the mixing of religion and politics." They point to research that shows that a majority of the public believes the Church should remain on the sidelines rather than address public issues. They add, "More than two-thirds believe that congregations should not endorse candidates for public office and that religious leaders should not try to imitate lobbyists by influencing public policy."[14]

How Christians can become involved in politics and remain faithful to Christ

Despite the challenges inherent in getting immersed in politics and remaining faithful to the teachings of scripture, Christians will continue to do so. This begs to the question: How is this possible? Here are four ideas:[15]

1. Pray for political leaders

Churches and individual Christians should consistently pray for political leaders—whether or not one agrees with the leaders' party affiliation, policies, faith or lack of it. To this point, pastors of many traditional evangelical churches usually offer a 'pastoral prayer' as part of every Sunday morning service. I attended such services for decades and was always moved as the pastor offered prayers for our elected leaders as well as prayers regarding major regional, national or international events. With the emergence of the independent, nondenominational church model—with its corresponding casual, guitar-led, simplistic music and worship style—these prayers have gone by the wayside. Of course, we should pray for our elected leaders at home, too.

That said, the Apostle Paul's admonition in 1 Timothy 2: 1-4 (NIV) could not be clearer:

> "I urge, then, first of all, that petitions, prayers, intercession and thanksgiving be made for all people—for kings and all those in authority, that we may live peaceful and quiet lives in all godliness and holiness. This is good, and pleases God our Savior, who wants all people to be saved and to come to a knowledge of the truth."

Prayers for leaders is of utmost importance. The term, "first of all" does not refer to the first in a list of items Paul wishes to enumerate. (No second or third items are mentioned.) Rather, "first of all" means first in importance. In today's parlance, Paul is saying, "In the first place—or most importantly—we need to pray for leaders, from the President on down."[16]

Also, Paul tells us that we should pray for "all those in authority." In the American context, this means that we should pray for leaders in all three branches of our government: the president and his or her team, the Supreme Court and our federal judges. And let's not forget our senators and congressmen/congresswomen. In addition, we are called on to pray for our state and city leaders—right down to school board members.

Next, the Apostle Paul urges us to offer all manner of prayers for our elected leaders. This includes asking God to grant specific things (petitions). We are challenged to make general requests (prayers) and specific, heartfelt requests on our leaders' behalf (intercession). In fact, Paul says we are to pray for the salvation of our leaders (if they do not already know the Lord). The Apostle says that God "wants all people to be saved and come to a knowledge of the truth."

We are also urged to offer thanks to God for our leaders. And that means thanking God for leaders whose positions we don't support!

Why should we offer prayers for our leaders? Paul gives us a two-fold answer. First, that we may live in peace, and second, that we will be godly and holy people. Paul says, "That we may live peaceful and quiet lives in all godliness and holiness."

As I mentioned before, this means we should pray for leaders we don't like or respect as well as leaders of the opposing party. Let's look at two important factors in this regard: First, we should pray for our leaders because of the positions they hold over us. Notice that Paul did not include the names of the top elected officials in the Roman world—even though he and his readers knew their names. Instead, Paul gave the titles. He said, " . . . kings and all those in authority." The point is clear: We should pray for our leaders because of the positions they hold over us.

Second, we should pray for our leaders because in a sense, their official actions are a way of serving God. In Romans 13: 1-7, Paul points out that God set rulers in place to punish evildoers and maintain order. In his book, *The Better Angels of Our Nature: Why Violence has Declined*, Steve Pinker traces the history of homicides in the history of the world. Among the elements he cited for restraining violence is government. He says, "A government is a good thing to have, because in a state of anarchy, people's self-interest, self-deception and fear of those shortcomings in others would lead to constant strife."[17]

Yet, prayer is only a starting point in how Christians can become involved in politics while fully honoring the Lord. Voting is another tool.

2. Vote

Most evangelical Christians believe it's their duty—and some would say, obligation—to vote for 'God-fearing' candidates. These are the candidates who individually, and with their affiliated party, represent the most 'Christian' viewpoints. And this is where the definition of 'godly' tends to take on different meanings based on race, culture and ideology. White evangelicals tend to view 'godly' political stances as matters like pro-life, pro-Israel and pro prayer in schools. But with Black evangelicals, issues like caring for the poor and downtrodden, affirmative action, anti-crime legislation, gun safety legislation and immigration top the 'godly' list. Of course, in a heartbeat, both sides will quote scriptures to support their views.

Yet, there is a lot more Christians can do to influence legislation, and the following option is a tried-and-proven way to do so.

3. Engage in peaceful activism

Peaceful activism has been one of the most powerful tools Christians have used to influence political leaders to pass laws that reflect justice, morality and the teachings of Scripture. As Redekop states, "Christians (should) speak when governments are unresponsive to the legitimate concerns of minorities and exploited individuals."[18]

In most of the major ethical/moral dilemmas faced by Western governments over the past 500 years, people of faith have entered the political arena to make their voices heard by governments. Here are two such endeavors—one in which people of faith prodded government to act at a high level, and another in which people on a grassroots level took action to change unjust laws.

The abolition of slavery in the British Commonwealth illustrates how people of faith applied pressure on the British Parliament until it finally agreed to abolish slavery in the British colonies. Slavery had been practiced in the British West Indies since the mid-16th century. But it wasn't until the late 18th century—more than 200 years later—that ending the slave trade and abolishing slavery began to be seriously challenged at the level where it mattered: the British Parliament.

The initial round of challenges to slavery began in England in 1772 when Granville Sharp, a brilliant young man and a person of faith, began a campaign to win the freedom of Black slaves in England. His efforts were largely successful. Sharp devoted his life to the cause of abolishing slavery and wrote a book detailing his anti-slavery views. The work garnered the attention of prominent leaders, including Pennsylvania Quaker Anthony Benezet, who had already published anti-slavery pieces. Popular Methodist evangelist John Wesley also made contact with Sharp as a result of the book. Wesley later became a staunch abolitionist.

Sharp's effort resulted in slavery ending in England on June 22, 1772, and Sharp became the father of the abolitionist movement.

Then, in 1784, the first organized attack on the British slave system took place when a group of Quakers, a Christian group otherwise known as the Society of Friends, circulated a pamphlet calling for freedom to "Oppressed Africans." The pamphlet was sent to every member of the British Parliament. It also influenced many others to join the abolitionist movement. Among the new recruits to the movement was a young, well-educated Christian firebrand named Thomas Clarkson. The group became known as the Clapham Sect, named for the wealthy London suburb where most of them lived.[19]

Christianity was the driving force behind the abolitionist movement. As historian R. N. Murray observes, "Together with William Wiberforce, they (the Clapham Sect) formed the Society for the Abolition of the Slave Trade. To the aim of abolishing the slave trade they added a desire, as religious men, to see Christian teaching extended to the Negroes."[20]

Like other members of the group, Clarkson devoted the

rest of his life to the abolitionist cause. Armed with firsthand information from fellow-abolitionists like Granville Sharp, Clarkson visited British slave ports including Liverpool in England. There, he boarded ships and gathered evidence, such as the crowded, shackled-filled, excrement-smelling conditions in which the slaves were forced to exist during the 'Middle Passage.' This is the Atlantic sea route from West Africa to the New World. Clarkson also took instruments used to torture slaves.

The leading mover and shaker in the abolitionist movement was William Wilberforce, the acknowledged leader of the Clapham Sect. Like the other abolitionists, Wilberforce's passion for the abolition of slaves grew out of his faith in Christ. In fact, Wilberforce's pastor was John Newton, the slave trader who was converted to Christianity and who wrote the famous hymn, *Amazing Grace, How Sweet The Sound*.

Wilberforce teamed up with his friend, Britain's Prime Minister William Pitt, to bring the issue of abolition before the British Parliament. Starting in 1789, Wilberforce introduced bills in the House of Commons to end the slave trade. The bills gained the support of fellow parliamentarian Charles Fox and Edmund Burke. But they failed to become enacted into law.

In the ensuing years, Wilberforce introduced legislation outlawing the slave trade and slavery itself, but the attempts were defeated. However, the abolitionist cause began to garner public support. In his 1792 bill, Wilberforce cited the support of hundreds of thousands of fellow English people who had signed petitions favoring the abolition of the slave trade.

Finally, in 1807, Parliament passed a law ending the slave trade. This move was historic. It meant that British ships would no longer visit West African ports with money and trinkets to lure African thugs to deliver men, women and even children to enter stinking ships to cross the Atlantic Ocean en route to the West Indies. An untold number of Africans lost their lives on this route, dying as a result of disease, torture, suicide or being thrown overboard to 'lighten' the ships' load during storms.

Now came the bigger battle: convincing Parliament to abolish slavery itself. Wilberforce, and other members of the Anti-Slavery Society, kept the pressure on Parliament. However, by this time, support for abolition was increasing in England. In fact, the Quakers and other groups sympathetic to the abolitionist cause presented the case for abolition in pulpits and public meetings, newspaper articles, pamphlets and posters. Also, some younger anti-slavery presenters (Wilberforce was old and frail by this time) presented petitions bearing nearly one and a half million signatures.

On August 28, 1833, a new day dawned for millions of enslaved people in the British colonies. Because on that day, Parliament passed the Slavery Abolition Act. With the stroke of the pen, more than 800,000 enslaved Africans in the Caribbean, South Africa and Canada became free. The law took effect on August 1, 1834.[21]

How long slavery would have lasted in the British colonies without the peaceful activism of the Anti-Slavery movement is anybody's guess. We know that several major slave revolts had taken place in French and British colonies leading up to emancipation. Also, Baptist, Moravian and Quaker missionaries played a major role in convincing the slaves not to rebel against their oppressors. But one thing is for certain: Christian people, motivated by the teachings of Jesus, used the political process as well as contemporary mass media to make their case before government until their goals were met.

Another approach to influence government to pass moral laws plays out with political activism at the grassroots level. The success of the Civil Rights movement in America is perhaps the best example in American history. On the one hand, one can view the Civil Rights Era as the historic social justice events bookended by the Brown v. Board of Education Supreme Court Ruling of 1954 and the Voting Rights Act of 1965. But another lens through which the Civil Right Era can be viewed is that Christian people—both Black and white—participated in political activism at the grassroots level until local, state and our national government passed laws that provided equality to all citizens.

The leadership of the Civil Rights movement was overwhelmingly Christian. Civil Rights leaders included Dr. Martin Luther King Jn., a Baptist minister; John Lewis, a Freedom Rider turned Baptist minister turned legendary US Congressman; Rosa Parks, African Methodist Episcopal

Church (AME) church member and activist whose refusal to move to the back of the bus sparked the Montgomery Bus Boycott (1955-1956); and Baptist minister Reverend Ralph Abernathy.[22]

Nonviolent resistance was a cornerstone of political activism carried out by the Civil Rights Movement. Dr. King advocated nonviolence as taught by Jesus and modeled by Indian leader Mahatma Gandhi.[23] As Juan Williams observes, "King's first uses of the nonviolent method were based more on the Bible and Christian pacifism than on the teachings of the Mahatma."[24]

In fact, the movement taught the tactics of nonviolent resistance at churches and other venues across the South. And the students learned their lessons well. Arguably the most famous display of the movement's nonviolent resistance took place during a series of demonstrations in Birmingham, Alabama, in 1963 to protest widespread segregation in the city.

Like many other metropolitan areas in the South, Birmingham had a sizable Black population. But only three people of color served on the city council. Most perplexing to the Black population was the fact that the business establishments in greater Birmingham all but excluded Blacks from employment and, through harassment and intimidation, from shopping and receiving services as well.

As a result, the Civil Rights Movement, under the direction of Dr. King, decided to conduct a massive demonstration in the city. This led some members of the movement to meticulously strategize how the demonstrations would proceed. The Sixteenth Street Baptist Church in Birmingham served as the nerve center of the demonstration. One leader went as far as to calculate how long it took for the average young person, middle-aged person and older participant to march from the church to the business district downtown. The leaders also pragmatically factored in who would demonstrate—and get themselves arrested—and who would stay out of jail. That way, they could arrange bail for the folks who were arrested. In fact, in preparation for the demonstrations, Dr. King went on a national speaking tour in which he gave 28 speeches in 16 cities and raised more than $75,000 to cover bail expenses for the anticipated arrests.

The white power brokers in Birmingham received wind of the pending demonstration and made preparations, too. Most notably, Bull Connor, a white supremacist who was in charge of the police force, cleared the jail cells as much as possible in preparation for thousands of demonstrators. And not to be outdone, Alabama governor George Wallace launched his term of office with the ominous statement, "Segregation now! Segregation tomorrow! Segregation forever!"

So, while the Black demonstrators—a large majority of whom were Christian—prepared to use the tools of peaceful activism, the white supremacist leaders in the city and state were ready to unleash their weapons which included fists, billy clubs, guns, firehoses—and snarling German Shepherd police dogs!

The first round of demonstrations began in early April

when 30 people took to the streets to peacefully demonstrate. They were promptly arrested. The following day, another group of demonstrators clashed with police officers. Dr. King, Reverend Abernathy and about 50 other demonstrators took to the streets and were arrested shortly thereafter. The civil rights leaders were thrown in jail. And during solitary confinement, Dr. King wrote his now famous *Letter from a Birmingham Jail*. Eight days after being locked up, Dr. King and Rev. Abernathy were released from jail. They immediately met with other members of the Southern Christian Leadership Conference (SCLC) to plan the next phase of the protest.

By this time, even some of the Black folks who were otherwise committed to the cause began to get discouraged. It was then that Civil Rights leader James Bevel presented his strategy: recruiting kids—from six to 18 years old—to participate in the protests. The leaders calculated that since the children and teenagers did not work, their families would not be economically disadvantaged if they protested. But the fact that parents allowed their kids to participate in such a risky endeavor indicated the degree of commitment and desperation the Black parents felt regarding their second-class status.

Leaving the movement's headquarters at Sixteenth Street Baptist Church, the children began their demonstration on a Thursday morning. Shortly thereafter, the police swooped in and began arresting the innocent kids. Under the command of the fuming, vengeful and heartless segregationist

Bull Connor, the police began herding the kids into paddy wagons. But they kept on marching and singing freedom songs. Bull Connor then brought in school buses to take the kids away. But they kept on coming. By the end of the day, 957 Black kids were spending the night in Birmingham jails.

The news spread to every corner of the country—including via television. Attorney General Robert Kennedy called King to make the case that the kids could get hurt by the police. Yet, the demonstrations continued. On the next day, more than 1,000 kids skipped school to join the protest. This time, Bull Connor decided to up the ante. He brought out police dogs and firehoses to suppress the demonstrators. The dogs mauled several demonstrators.

Equally detestable, Connor's thugs, with firehoses in hand, trained the powerful stream of water that can rip the bark off trees to take down the kids. "Children were knocked down by the streams, slamming into curbs and over parked cars,"[25] writes Juan Williams. The pressure of the water smacked children to the ground and sent them rolling down the street like soda cans spinning in a gutter.

Still, the protest grew. By the following Monday, more than 2,000 marchers were incarcerated. Some were placed in Birmingham jails, others in a makeshift prison at the Alabama state fairgrounds.

As expected, the horrific news of the protest became the top stories in radio and television newscasts plus newspapers across the USA and around the world. The Alabama governor dispatched 500 state officers and members of the National Guard to maintain order.

Finally, the demonstrations began to abate. President Kennedy sent Assistant Attorney General, Burke Marshall, to negotiate between Dr. King and Birmingham's city leaders. Due to the overwhelming impact of the protests, King told Marshall that Blacks wanted to be integrated into every aspect of the life of the city. But the two men decided to start by demanding the desegregation of lunch counters in Birmingham's downtown stores. After lengthy negotiations, the city merchants decided to desegregate the lunch counters and hire Black employees as sales associates and clerical staff.

Meanwhile, the KKK bombed the hotel where Dr. King had been staying. Rioting erupted, and Connor's forces as well as state troopers moved in. In response, President Kennedy sent soldiers from a nearby military base to maintain order.

On June 19, a mere two months after the Birmingham protests started, President Kennedy delivered a new Civil Rights Bill to Congress. The bill's provisions included:

- Outlawing segregation in all interstate public accommodations,
- Allowing the attorney general to file suits demanding school integration,
- Giving the attorney general the power to stop funding federal programs in which discrimination occurred, and

- Initiatives to ensure the right to vote by declaring that persons who have a sixth-grade education would be presumed to be literate.

To help ensure that the Civil Rights Bill would not languish in Congress, a number of civil rights organizations united in planning a March on Washington. On August 28, 1963, more than 250,000 people—including about 60,000 white people and tens of thousands of church members of all races—converged in the Washington Mall for the historic occasion. Dr. King delivered the now famous *I Have a Dream* speech.

A positive change for Black people was in the air. On July 2, 1964, President Lyndon Johnson signed the historic Civil Rights Acts of 1964.[26]

Peaceful activism won!

Taking to the streets in order to influence political leaders to take action remains a powerful tool even today. In fact, following the police killing of George Floyd in 2020, an estimated 15 to 26 million people demonstrated across America and millions more worldwide. In the words of a *New York Times* headline, "Black Lives Matter May Be the Largest Movement in U.S. History."[27] Whether peaceful activism focuses on civil rights, racial equality, pro-life issues or some other just cause, this form of protest is a tried-and-proven means for passionate people representing all walks of life to enter the political arena and make their cases known to the powers that be.

Or, as Redekop reminds us,

"As Christians, we ought to remind our rulers that they are accountable to God. Our rulers need to know that both as individuals and as governments, they are ultimately accountable to a sovereign God. They need to hear that someday they will answer to Him for how they lived their personal lives, as well as for how they used the power and authority He delegated to them. There is a Prime Minister of prime ministers, a King of kings, and a President of presidents, who will someday call them to account."[28]

Yet, there is one more way in which Christians can immerse themselves in politics and remain faithful to Christ. Although, this involvement calls for an extra measure of resolve.

4. Participate as elected officials

Every career has its fair share of demands and temptations that potentially lure even the most committed Christian from his or her devotion to Christ. Accountants may be tempted to 'cook' the books. Investment professionals can be drawn to insider trading or making investments using clients' securities. Marketers might lie by overstating product benefits, and police officers can be tempted to plant or otherwise falsify evidence in order to catch a criminal. The list goes on.

But politics strikes me as one of those fields that poses special challenges because issues like agreeing with party positions—even when they are mean-spirited or immoral—are baked into the equation. It's no secret that failing to abide by the party line can result in 'getting primaried'—losing the party nomination to vie for elected office or being voted out of office. Even if a candidate wins, he or she can forfeit a powerful committee position by failing to abide by the party line.

For example, Republican congress people and senators largely supported Trump's agenda—including labeling immigrants as criminals, demeaning Black and Brown people, separating nursing babies from their mothers who are seeking asylum and turning a blind eye to Trump's profiting off his presidency in violation of the Emolument's Clause.

Also, in general terms, Republicans, in their quest for fiscal restraint, have the propensity to limit funding to the most vulnerable citizens while giving tax breaks to the wealthy. Trump's massive tax cut to millionaires and billionaires is a case in point. In addition, many Christians believe that the GOP systematically refuses to tighten gun laws despite the epidemic of mass shootings. Some Christians believe this represents the GOP's callous disregard for human life—their 'pro-life' stance notwithstanding.

On the Democratic side, Christian legislators are expected to line up behind positions that followers of Jesus traditionally consider to be sinful. I am referring to matters like same-sex marriage and most positions on abortion.

Indeed, it seems as if only seasoned politicians seem to be free to simply vote their conscience. In this regard, the late Republican Senator John McCain and Senator Joe Manchin come to mind. In 2018, Senator McCain defied his Republican colleagues by casting the deciding vote to save the Affordable Care Act (Obamacare). In similar vein, in 2021, Senator Manchin, as the sole hold-out, refused to back a scaled-down version of President Biden's Build Back Better bill, thereby scuttling it.

Over the years, I have written to and received responses from elected leaders representing both parties. I have been amused and angered by their responses—amused because their words mirror the talking points I hear from their party leaders. And I am angered because the congressional representatives and senators appear to think that I am so stupid that I will accept their incoherent, illogical, pass-the-buck excuses for the positions they take.

So, are there any past or current elected officials in Washington, D.C. whose personal lifestyle and positions on issues uncompromisingly reflect the teachings of Christ? I can think of a few individuals representing both major political parties who fit the bill. But citing their names might stir an unwinnable debate. I am positive that Christians can successfully reflect the teachings of Christ despite the potential pitfalls of the political process. My optimism is based on the story of Daniel in the Old Testament. You probably remember the story from Sunday school or prophetic Bible studies. Let's take a new look at the

Christians Involve Themselves in Politics? | 179

story through the lens of a believer's involvement in wordy politics:

In about 586 B.C., Nebuchadnezzar, king of Babylon, besieges the city of Jerusalem and takes thousands of the Israeli people back to Babylon as captives. (Babylon is present-day Iraq.) Among the captives are four young men—Daniel, Shadrach, Meshach and Abednego. Bible scholars believe the boys were between 13 and 17 years old at the time. On the king's orders, the chief of staff selects the four guys to undergo special training to become civil servants in Babylon. The guys undergo a three-year training program in the language, literature and culture of Babylon.

They are offered special food and wine similar to what is served to the king. But Daniel refuses to eat the food because he considers it a defilement of his body. He asks for permission not to eat the king's food. The chief of staff honors the request, and Daniel and his friends are put on a vegetarian diet for 10 days. After that time, they are deemed to be in better shape than their peers who ate the king's food. As a result, they're allowed to continue their diet.

At the end of the three years, Nebuchadnezzar interviews the young men and finds them to be superior in wisdom and understanding than the magicians and enchanters in Babylon. So, they all enter the king's service. Nebuchadnezzar has a disturbing dream, and his wise men, enchanters, magicians and diviners are unable to recount the dream or interpret it. Daniel recounts the dream and offers an interpretation. Daniel gives credit to God for giving him the interpretation. The king in turn praises Daniel for giving him the interpretation. He also honors Daniel's God as "the God of gods, the Lord of kings and a revealer of mysteries," (Daniel 2:46).

The king appoints Daniel as ruler over the entire province of Babylon. As such, Daniel serves in the king's royal court, where he supervises the king's wise men. At Daniel's request, his three friends—Shadrach, Meshach and Abednego—become administrators over the province of Babylon.

Nebuchadnezzar builds a massive statue and demands that everyone bows down and worship the statue at the sound of an array of musical instruments. Failure to do so will result in being thrown into a blazing furnace. The three young men refuse to bow in worship, and their refusal catches the attention of the king's astrologers. Word gets back to the king, who orders the lads to bow to the statue. The guys politely tell the king that they cannot do so. They add that they know God can save them. But even if God does not save them from being burned to death, they still will not bow to anyone or anything other than God. The boys are thrown into the furnace. Nebuchadnezzar watches. He sees not three, but four figures walking amid the flames. The fourth person is none other than the pre-incarnate Christ. The king once again praises God for saving the three brave young men and gives them promotions.

The king receives a second dream and Daniel once again gives an interpretation. Nebuchadnezzar's great kingdom will fall, and he will live a desperate life for seven years.

About 47 years after Daniel was taken to Babylon, Nebuchadnezzar's grandson, Belshazzar, serves as co-regent (judge or regent) of Babylon. The mighty, well-fortified city of Babylon is under siege by the Medes and Persians. Yet, Belshazzar throws a party involving thousands of the country's nobles, their wives and concubines. He even uses the gold and silver goblets Nebuchadnezzar stole from Israel decades earlier. But the people aren't praising Jehovah. Rather, "they praised the gods of gold and silver, of bronze, iron, wood and stone," (Daniel 5:4 NIV).

Suddenly a large hand appears against a wall, and a finger writes an ominous message that no one in the large hall can decipher. The king and his top leaders are horrified. In desperation, the king summons Daniel, who is a senior citizen by this time, to interpret the writing on the wall. The king offers Daniel a position next in line to himself plus riches if he successfully interprets the writing. Daniel tells Belshazzar that due to his arrogance and allegiance to pagan gods, he will lose his kingdom to the Medes and Persians.

Belshazzar clothes Daniel in the finest garments, adorns his neck with a gold chain and proclaims him second in command. But the promotion is short lived. Hours later, Darius the Mede takes over the kingdom. Darius appoints three leaders to run the country with him, and Daniel becomes one of these leaders. Daniel outshines the other two leaders because of his 'excellent spirit.' Evidently, he exhibits a superb attitude toward life, his work and relationships with others.

As can be expected, Daniel's positive attitude and stellar record of accomplishments make him the object of attack. Daniel's enemies try as hard as they can to find a flaw in his conduct, administrative style or work history in order to bring him down. But they find nothing. In fact, the only 'shortcoming' they can find with Daniel relates to his devotion to God.

So, the enemies of Daniel concoct a plan to destroy him once and for all. They butter up to King Darius and ask him to issue a mandate that anyone who prays to any god or human being except the king during the next 30 days will be thrown into the lions' den. King Darius puts the decree into writing.

Daniel learns of the decree but maintains his devotional life. He goes home to his upstairs room where the windows are open toward Jerusalem. He gets down on his knees and prays to God. He does this three times a day—just as he did for decades. Daniel's enemies catch him in the act and report him to the king.

Reluctantly, the king orders Daniel to be placed into the den filled with hungry lions. The king says to Daniel, "May your God, whom you serve continually, rescue you!" (Daniel 6:16 NIV).

Early the next morning, the king hurries to the den and asks Daniel if God rescued him. Daniel replies that, indeed, God *did* shut the mouths of lions, leaving him unharmed. The king orders that Daniel be taken out of the lions' den. He issues a decree that "in every part of my kingdom, people must fear and reverence the God of Daniel," (Daniel 6:26 NIV).

The story of Daniel provides three major lessons concerning being faithful to God in the world of secular politics.

a. Christians in politics should remain faithful to God even at the cost of their careers

Daniel and his three friends decided from the get-go that they would not do or say anything that would defile their bodies or in any way conflict with their faith in God. Despite being chosen to receive training for civil service of the great country of Babylon, the boys decided not to partake of the king's food and drinks. The food represented more than nutrition. It spoke to the boys' relationship with God. In the words of David Guzik, pastor of Calvary Chapel in Santa Barbara, California, "First, it (the food) undoubtedly was not kosher. Second, it was probably sacrificed to idols. Third, eating the king's food implied fellowship with Babylon's cultural system."[29]

Later, Daniel's three friends—Shadrach, Meshach and Abednego—refused to bow down to the huge golden image that Nebuchadnezzar had set up even though they knew that doing so could result in their being killed. For Nebuchadnezzar, the boys' refusal to bow was an act of treason. Like politicians before and after him, Nebuchadnezzar conflated spiritual and national allegiances. But the Jewish boys did not accept such a cult of personality.

In our current political system, no one is demanding that we worship a statue (although a golden statue of Donald Trump was unveiled at the 2021 Conservative Political Action Conference—CPAC—in Orlando, Fla., attended by white evangelical leaders).[30] However, given the current status of GOP politics, multitudes of Christians in America have become part of Trump's personality cult. In campaign rallies, Trump did something never done before in American politics: He asked his followers to make a personal allegiance to HIM—not the Republican party, not democracy, not the United States—to HIM![31]

In the lead up to the 2020 elections, the Republican Party made an unprecedented move. The party decided to forgo drafting a Party Platform—a formal document outlining the positions supported by the party, which will become the basis on which the party appeals to the public for support. Instead, the party leadership used the COVID pandemic as a cover and agreed to "enthusiastically support the President's America-first agenda" in lieu of the traditional platform.[32]

Christians who still follow Trump and Trumpism are turning a blind eye to the clear teachings of Jesus by accepting practices like lies, slander, sexual immorality and stealing (including classified documents) as normative.

Christians must refuse to bow to any cult of personality!

Following the teachings of Christ in the world of politics also means refraining from other forms of defilement—such as taking bribes and kickbacks and/or lying about party positions—yours or your opponents.' In short, any practice that sullies the name of Christ in the name of political expedience must be off the table for Christians who hold political office.

b. Christians must practice the highest levels of honesty and integrity in their political careers

Perhaps no career is as 'public' as those of elected officials. They are called upon to make big decisions about people's lives, money, health and safety. Constituents and the media, friends and foes alike, follow elected leaders' positions on any number of issues. And they are quick to praise or criticize a politician's position at every turn.

For these reasons, it is incumbent on elected leaders who are also followers of Christ to apply honesty, integrity and morality to every move they make, and the biblical account of Daniel and his three friends illustrate this point perfectly.

After Daniel, Shadrach, Meshach and Abednego completed their three-year civil service training program, King Nebuchadnezzar interviewed them and found them to be superior in wisdom and understanding compared to the magicians and enchanters in the kingdom. Then, after Daniel interpreted Nebuchadnezzar's first dream, the four young men passed another level of scrutiny. The king gave Daniel a higher position, which included authority over the other advisers. In addition, the king appointed Shadrach, Meshach and Abednego to the position of administrators over the province of Babylon.

Decades later, when Daniel's enemies tried to trap him

after King Darius gave Daniel kudos for being his top regional leader, they could not find a single fault with Daniel's conduct, administrative skills or decisions. In this regard, Guzik observes, "Imagine looking as hard as you can at a public servant in office some 50 years and finding *nothing wrong*. No fraudulent expense accounts. No intern scandals. No questionable business deals. No gifts from lobbyists. No accusations from his staff . . . Simply, there were no skeletons in Daniel's closet. His enemies examined his life and found nothing to attack—so they had to make up something."[33]

Let that sink in. Daniel was a foreigner who was captured and trained to serve in Babylon. His personal life and his work were so exemplary that the only 'fault' his enemies could find related to his faith in God. This is how Christians who serve in politics should act—meticulous, efficient and results-oriented while being honest, moral and just. All the time, year in and year out!

c. God should get the glory from a Christian's work in politics

Many people within and outside the world of politics believe that public service in its purest form is God's work. They cite Jesus words that we are supposed to be 'salt' and light' in and to the world (Matthew 5:13-16). They point to Romans 13, where the Apostle Paul says that God established government to protect and preserve society at large. Still others point to Micah 6:8, where the prophet asks us to 'live out' justice, mercy and humility: "And what does the Lord require of you? To act justly and to love mercy and to walk humbly with your God," (NIV).

Indeed, the practical aspects of government take the form of positive values like safety, peace, provision for those in need, compensation for the oppressed plus justice for those who are wronged. Who can argue that these values do not glorify God?

That said, the method of achieving these positive results should also bring glory to the Lord. Time and again, the leaders of Babylon were so impressed with the faith, conduct and actions of Daniel and his friends that they gave glory to the Lord.

After King Nebuchadnezzar had his first dream, Daniel offered to interpret the dream. Then, Daniel asked God to reveal the dream and its interpretation to him, and he asked his three friends to join with him in praying about the matter. That night, God revealed the vision and its meaning to Daniel, and he told this to the king. In response to hearing the dream and its interpretation, the king said, "Surely your God is the God of gods and the Lord of kings and a revealer of mysteries, for you were able to reveal this mystery," (Daniel 2:37 NIV).

When Shadrach, Meshach and Abednego were thrown in the furnace, the king, believing that God might save them, peeked in as saw them alive and walking around amid the flames. After witnessing the miracle and ordering that the guys be taken out of the furnace, Nebuchadnezzar exclaimed,

"Praise be to the God of Shadrach, Meshach and Abednego, who has sent his angel and rescued his servants!" (Daniel 3:28 NIV).

After Daniel's life was miraculously spared in the lions' den, Scripture records that King Darius issued a decree "to all the nations and peoples of every language in all the earth . . . that in every part of my kingdom people must fear and reverence the God of Daniel," (Daniel 6:25-26 NIV).

The political activities of Daniel and his friends and their faith in God resulted in Babylon learning that God was at work. Wouldn't it be great if Christian lawmakers in America would live out their faith to the degree that miraculous breakthroughs happen in the legislative process and that God would get the glory? Wouldn't it be spectacular if Christian lawmakers would be able to say on national television that they witnessed God's hand in particular legislation? I am not advocating for a theocracy. I am simply saying that when Christians bring their faith to the legislative process, and when millions of Christians join in prayer for godly outcomes, breakthroughs can occur in which God gets the glory!

This is how Christians should get involved in the political process—by voting, praying for political leaders, engaging in peaceful activism and by participating as elected officials!

Part 4

It's Time to Make Christ Lord of the Church

But we are citizens of heaven, where the Lord Jesus Christ lives. And we are eagerly waiting for him to return as our Savior.

Philippians 3:20 (NLT)

Chapter 11

The Church's Job: Agents of Reconciliation

Years ago, shortly after I became a certified scuba diver, I dived an underwater park in the upper Florida Keys. And I learned an important spiritual lesson. Back then, I was not confident about my underwater navigation skills. So, I accompanied three other divers on a dive-master-led tour of the reef. The sandy bottom was about 25 feet—very shallow for scuba diving—and the visibility was perfect. Despite wearing dive gear, I felt like I wasn't swimming, but enjoying a leisurely walk in the park. We meandered through one beautiful coral formation after the other. Fish zoomed by inches in front of my mask—like cars on the freeway. I also saw moray eels lurking among the coral plus hammerhead and reef sharks as well as turtles effortlessly swimming by—or resting on the white sand.

Because I was not leading the dive, I did not bother to check my compass for the direction we were taking. But I kept track of my 'bottom time' (how long I was submerged) and my air supply. Almost an hour had elapsed, and I noticed that my air was getting low. So, I signaled to the divemaster that we needed to get back to the boat. He signaled that we should remain on the sandy bottom while he surfaced to look for the direction of the boat. The divemaster slowly ascended and returned a few minutes later. Then, he gave us the 'go' signal, held his console in his extended hands and followed his compass. Soon, we saw the boat's anchor line, where we surfaced.

Granted, we were never in jeopardy. We could have easily surfaced at any time and done a surface swim back to the boat, about the length of a soccer field away. But that would have been embarrassing. ('Real' divers know how to navigate underwater.) In reality, we were lost among the picturesque reefs. But we did the smart thing. The divemaster moved out of the elements that kept us lost so he could get a clear sight of where we all needed to go.

My lost-among-the-reef experience is a metaphor of where the white evangelical Church in America has found itself today. If the Church is not supposed to wander around in the world of right-wing politics, conspiracy theories and divisive political allegiances, where is it supposed to be, and how does it get there? Let's rise above the reef and find out.

Before we find our path to where we should be as a Church, let's explore where the white evangelical Church is at present. The Church has become part of the Republican party machine. And the Church is using this affiliation to bring about 'spiritual' aims such as preserving life (through less abortions), preserving the institution of marriage (through attempts to overturn same-sex marriage laws) and growing the influence of the Christian Church (through restricting immigration from Muslim countries). Stated differently, the white Church is seeking to 'save America' by becoming a political force.

In this regard, Campbell observes, "To many today, evangelicals are perceived as politically power-hungry, gun-toting, Trump-supporting white nationalists, and their ability to speak of Christ's message of reconciliation, peace, love and equality is muted by other messages."[1]

Let's consider three reasons the Church should not unite with a political party—any political party—and become a political force:

1. Worldly politics is diametrically opposed to the character and mission of the Church

In the Bible, the primary Greek word used for the Church is ekklesia. In Greek society, this term was used to describe people who were 'called out' from their regular lives to serve on the town council. In fact, the council was called ekklesia. (Greece is considered to be the birthplace of democracy.) But, as pointed out in *Introductory Lectures in Systematic Theology*, "The New Testament has filled it (the term ekklesia) with a spiritual content, so that it means a people called out from the world and from sinful things.[2]

To this point, pastor Andy Stanley notes:

"Saving America is not the mission of the Church. The moment our love or concern for country takes precedence over our love for the people in our country, we are off mission. When saving America diverts energy, focus and reputation away from saving Americans, we no longer qualify as the ekklesia (the 'called out' ones) of Jesus. We're merely political tools. A manipulated voting demographic . . . Again, we lose our elevated position as the conscience of the nation. We give up the moral and ethical high ground."[3]

Is the growing nondenominational movement in America more interested in amassing members than acting like the ekklesia—a people 'called out' from the world? Last summer, my wife and I visited the tiny South Bass Island in Lake Erie. On our drive home, we took a foray into Michigan and visited a church in a small town. We arrived there just in time for Sunday morning service.

The pastor spent his entire sermon bragging about how his congregation is being 'relevant' by reaching out to football players on the town's high school team and also to members of the police force. Then, the pastor said, "Some people ask me 'what's the size of your congregation?'" (There were probably 150 people in the room.) "I tell them 10,000," he continued. "Because that's the size of our town. And our mission is to minister to every person in this town."

This pastor conflated the missionizers—the church—and the mission field—the world. So, to him, the church and the world are one and the same. As God's people here on earth, we're totally different from the world. Our allegiance should be solely to Christ. Our goal is holiness. Our 'boasting' is not about the size of our congregation but in our identification with the cross of Christ (Galatians 6:14). And the world does not share such an identification.

Indeed, the Church seems to have traded in the 'called out from the world' card for the 'join the world for political power' card. Rev. Ed Trevors, Rector of the Parish of St. Margaret of Scotland, in Halifax, Nova Scotia, Canada, berates the white evangelical Church for embracing Donald Trump in order to gain political power. He says,

> "Trump was supposed to usher in a Golden Age where the evangelical Church would finally have that political power that was promised to them when they took this particular path back in the mid-late seventies . . . The government was finally going to bow its knee to them."

Trevors claims that Trump failed to deliver that Golden Age, and as a result, church leaders are now whining that Trump 'used them.' The Anglican pastor points out that the Church in America is paying a huge cost for affiliating itself with Trump.

"When churches go after that worldly authority, there is a cost. And that cost is much more than just our support in the moment." Trevors asserts that the white Church in America "pointed their congregations to Trump" by saying,

> "'Yes, all these problems of the world? Trump can fix that . . . However, in doing so, the Church 'literally pointed people away from Christ.' They said, 'put your hope there—not on the cross. Put your hope in them (Trump and the GOP)—not on Jesus. Count on them to give you what you want, not on Jesus to do that. Count on them to provide for the things that you need, not on counting on Jesus to do that.'"

Trevors asserts that by aligning with Trump, pastors forfeited their ability to lead and guide their own flocks. He adds, "They're following the messiah that the evangelical churches held up a replacement for Jesus Christ."

Trevors warns that the ultimate cost of the Church following Trump is that, "It will be almost impossible for them (the pastors) to bring those people home."[4]

2. Alignment with worldly politics forces the Church to defend the indefensible

At the beginning of this book, I mentioned that my friend, Maggie, embraces Trumpism to the degree that she excuses his vile conduct and terrible positions. Embracing the MAGA agenda calls for Christians to defend indefensible positions—from white supremacy to antisemitism, sexual assault to fraud, lying to stealing, inflammatory rhetoric to insurrection.

On this subject, Rev. Trevors points out that Republican congresswoman Marjorie Taylor Green advocates unfounded conspiracy theories, such as the claim that Jewish[5] space lasers are starting the California wildfires[6] and that right-wing Christians are forced to defend this type of antisemitism: "And when she starts spewing off about Jewish space lasers, the Christians that are out there in the world who are trying to share the loving message about Jesus Christ, they now have to answer for, 'Didn't your person rail against Jewish space lasers?'".

3. Alignment with worldly politics hinders the Church from objectively presenting the gospel

Our mission as the Church is to call people to faith in Christ. Or, in the words of the Apostle Paul, be agents of reconciliation. The better job we do of getting people to become born-again believers who follow the teachings of Christ, the more 'Christian' America will become. However, as Jasmine Alnutt, professor at Calvary Chapel Bible College observes, "Anything that distracts the Church from its true purpose—obeying the Great Commission and preaching the Gospel—will eventually do more harm than good."[7]

Pastor Andy Stanley cuts to the chase by pointing out that with America roughly equally divided between Republicans and Democrats, aligning with the Republican party compromises our witness. "We systematically alienate more than half the souls in America through our un-Christlike rhetoric and fear-based posturing," he says.[8]

In 1 Corinthians 5: 17-20, Paul makes three important points about our status and responsibility as Christians. First, he says that Christians are 'new creations' through the work of Christ on the cross: "Therefore, if anyone is in Christ, the new creation has come: The old has gone, the new is here!" Christians are indwelled by the Holy Spirit. As a result, we have the power to be victorious over sin and to live a supernatural, Christ-like and exemplary life here on earth (Acts 1:8).

Second, Paul points out that "we are . . . Christ's ambassadors." When we become a Christian, our 'nationality' changes, in that our earthly citizenship (America, Canada, Jamaica, etc.) becomes secondary to our new, heavenly citizenship. Stated differently, from God's standpoint, because of our faith in Christ, we're primarily heavenly citizens and secondarily US citizens (or whichever country holds our citizenship).

Social scientist John H. Redekop notes, "All Christians are sisters and brothers in the Lord before we are citizens of any given country . . . In God's kingdom, family ties trump patriotism!"[9]

As heavenly citizens, we also have a job—that of being Christ's ambassador here on earth. To this point, Andy Stanley observes, "Christians are heaven's ambassadors, and our churches are its embassies . . . We represent this heavenly and future kingdom now."¹⁰ This means that we represent the values of the one who sent us: God himself. How well are we representing the principles, plans and objectives of God here on earth?

This brings us to Paul's third point in this passage: "We implore you on Christ's behalf: Be reconciled to God." The word, 'you' in the text was added by the translators. To put Paul's words into today's speech, we might say, "We urge everyone in America (or wherever you live) on Christ's behalf to be reconciled to God."

So, Church, that's our mission: present the message of reconciliation so unbelievers are brought to faith in Christ and then discipled to lead others to Christ also. As Christ commissioned us in Matthew 28: 19-20:

> "Go and make disciples of all nations, baptizing them in the name of the Father and of the Son and of the Holy Spirit, and teaching them to obey everything I have commanded you. And surely I am with you always, to the very end of the age."

Chapter 12
The Church's Goal: Reflect Heavenly Values

Several large cities across the USA have a Chinatown. In these self-sustaining enclaves, everything in the community is reminiscent of China: languages, stores, customs, architecture, schools, places of worship, social clubs, professional services, parks, hospitals and the like. As a result, it is possible for people to live their entire lives in Chinatown without leaving their community, if they so choose.

Chinatowns are essentially colonies of China in the United States. In similar fashion, every evangelical church should reflect their 'homeland'—heaven—in the way the church acts. And every church member should do the same.

In his letter to the church in Philippi, the Apostle Paul tells the believers, "We are citizens of heaven, where the Lord Jesus Christ lives. And we are eagerly waiting for him to return as our Savior," (Philippians 3:20 NLT).

Three points jump out at me from this text: First, as Christians, our primary allegiance is to heaven and its values. In his commentary on this text, David Guzik points out that Paul's injunction must have meant a lot to the church in Phillippi, since they "greatly valued their Roman citizenship."[1] Guzik says, "Just as the Philippians could consider themselves citizens of Rome and were under Roman laws and customs (even though they were in fact far from Rome) so Christians should consider themselves citizens of heaven."[2]

The message is clear. As believers, our home is in heaven. As a result, we are a colony of heaven here on earth. This means our primary allegiance is to heaven and its values, and our allegiance to the United States (or any other country) is secondary.

So, before we take a deep dive into political ideology—left-wing, center or right-wing—we must remember to weigh our political views and the person or persons we follow against the standards of heaven. Are our views pure, loving and for the betterment of people as a whole? Or are they degrading, divisive, racist or evil? Do the person or persons we follow reflect godly values in their personal lives and relationships with others?

The second thought that arises from the Philippians 3:20 text is that our ultimate goal in life should be accruing treasures in heaven, not building a kingdom here on earth. I am not advocating that we should be—as the saying goes—'so heavenly minded that we are no earthly good.' Rather, as citizens of heaven, we are well advised to focus on calling people to faith in Christ and discipling them in the faith. So, we need to figure out if we are really called to be part of an earthy political machine—especially one that is based on fulfilling the goals of a narcissistic leader.

The third, and perhaps the most important concept that arises from the Philippines 3:20 text is that as citizens of heaven, we—Christians—are different from 'earthly' citizens. And we need to act that way. To quote Guzik:

"If we are citizens of heaven, it means that we are resident aliens on earth. Foreigners are distinct in whatever foreign land they go. Christians must be so marked by their heavenly citizenship that they are noticed as different."[3]

As citizens of heaven, we love rather than hate. We unite rather than divide. We do good works even when no one else knows about it. We recognize our brotherhood/sisterhood in Christ with other believers above their racial or political identities.

Although I have lived in the United States for decades and am a naturalized US citizen, at some level I still recall every day that I am an immigrant from Jamaica. And I find myself subconsciously thinking that I need to make my native land 'proud' by the way I behave each day.

But more importantly, I am *always* aware that I must make my 'real homeland'—heaven—'proud' every single day by acting more and more like Jesus.

You could say each of us as Christians have a mission: to properly represent our King and his kingdom. In this regard, a hymn I sang in church when I was a child comes to mind. The first verse and refrain go like this:

> I am a stranger here, within a foreign land;
> My home is far away, upon a golden strand;
> Ambassador to be of realms beyond the sea,
> I'm here on business for my King.

> This is the message that I bring,
> A message angels fain would sing:
> "Oh, be ye reconciled,"
> Thus saith my Lord and King,
> "Oh, be ye reconciled to God."[4]

As citizens of heaven and ambassadors for Christ, the most powerful nation-changing activity we as members of the Church can become involved in is following Jesus in the truest sense of the word. To quote Campbell, "As ambassadors of Christ, we must demonstrate love and acceptance. This should be the loudest message that people hear from the Church. But that is rarely the case."[5] Campbell adds, "Love for our neighbor reaches across ethnic lines and extends to those who are different from us. It reaches those who may despise us or mistreat us."[6]

This 'citizens of heaven' approach to living the Christian life—in which loving our neighbors as ourselves is a key part of our daily life—is crucial to changing America for the better. Consider the Early Church. It certainly did not have political power. Yet, all accounts indicate that Christianity grew in the Roman world because Christians showed love for their neighbors. In fact, as Campbell notes,

> "They (Christians in the early Roman Empire) simply went about their business being salt and light in the world and making disciples of all nations. And their good deeds commended them to the skeptics around them. Christians became so well-known for their care of the poor that Emperor Julian the Apostate lamented in AD 362 how they made the Romans look bad."[7]

Campbell urges the Church in America to follow the example of the Early Church and practice love for our neighbors—manifested through kindness and good deeds. He says,

> "We should relinquish the false hope of winning the culture through political discipleship and (instead) focus on making disciples of Jesus. Christians should be known less for self-seeking political fervor and famous for our service to others. In these ways, evangelicals will again bring glory to God. And—who knows?—they might actually win over the culture without trying."[8]

What should your church and mine look like? No matter if our church is small or large, rural or urban, rich or poor, or any other demographic difference you can think of, it should be the kind of church that practices the type of Christianity where unbelievers and even skeptics look on us and our churches and say, "They're so much like Jesus, the church is like a mini-heaven—right here on earth."

On October 2, 2006, Charles Roberts IV, a 32-year-old milk tanker truck driver, entered an Amish 'one-room' schoolhouse in rural Lancaster County, Penna. Armed with a 9mm handgun, Roberts killed five Amish girls and wounded five other girls before turning the gun on himself. A Christian group that's part of the Anabaptist tradition, the Amish live a 'simple lifestyle' which most often includes farming plus trades like carpentry. The Amish are also non-resistant. They refrain from bearing arms for defense and do not participate in the military.

The nation was stunned by the savagery of the murders and by the Amish response. Amish men in the community were heard telling their young relatives not the hate the killer. Others lamented the fact that the shooter left a wife, Marie, small children and a mother. Amish members visited Marie and members of her family, extending forgiveness to them. An Amish man comforted the shooter's father for close to an hour. Scores of Amish folk attended the shooter's funeral and hugged members of the killer's family. Also, Marie was invited to one of the funerals—an unusual act for members of the closed group. In addition, the Amish community set up a charitable fund for the family of the shooter. And Amish folk donated money to Marie and her three children.

The Church's Goal: Reflect Heavenly Values | 207

Marie Roberts wrote an open letter to her Amish neighbors thanking them for their forgiveness, grace and mercy. The forgiveness, love, compassion and reconciliation extended to Charles Roberts, his wife and her family shocked the nation. It was a main topic of discussion on network TV shows and in major newspapers for weeks afterwards. Several mental health experts were interviewed on national media. Some claimed that the Amish people forgave the shooter too early. They hinted that doing so trivialized the horror of the murders.

But the response of the Amish to the senseless murders and injuries to their innocent kids should not have been seen as unusual. I say this because the Amish, as followers of Jesus, were simply acting as Jesus, our Savior and Lord, showed us how to act. Christians love those who act meanly toward them. Christians forgive even the most horrendous actions taken against them. Christians go the extra mile in extending grace and mercy.

Christians act—or should act—like Jesus. Every day. All the time. Irrespective of our careers or stations in life. So, what is Christ's charge to the Church in America—including the white Church, the Black Church and the Church representing a myriad of immigrant groups? Reflect Christ so much that the world says that we act so much like Jesus, we're like a colony of heaven.

How can today's evangelical church in America truly reflect Christ every day so the world sees us a part of a mini heaven here on earth? A good place to start is by repenting and confessing our sins. Millions of us need to do so!

Such a large-scale event might well spark a revival. That's what happened on Feb. 8, 2023, on the campus of Asbury University in Wilmore, Kentucky.

It all started as a routine Wednesday morning chapel service. After the official service was over, the students did not leave for class, labs, the sports fields, dorms or the cafeteria. Instead, they stayed. They prayed. And they worshiped.

Then, one of the students openly confessed some of his sins. And the mood changed. An increasing number of students kept on praying and worshipping.

Soon, word began to spread, and people started coming to the Asbury campus. By Wednesday evening, the outpouring of the Spirt began attracting college students from "hundreds of other colleges and universities,"[9]

On its website, Asbury University reports that news of the "outpouring" spread around the world. The university says that the event brought people from "as far away as Russia and Japan" to the campus. Also, a plethora of media outlets converged in Wilmore to cover the event. "Countless reports of life change, salvation and rededications to Christ were some of the amazing results of the Outpouring event," says the university website.[10]

The scope of the Asbury revival—as some media outlets called it—was enormous. The event attracted some 15,000 people each day, and about 50,000 to 70,000 people visited Wilmore[11], which has a population of just 6,000! In addition, the website Thir.st reported that a week after the revival broke out, "Videos under the hashtag #asburyrevival . . . garnered a total of 727.8 million views and counting on TikTok."[12]

Wow!

Imagine what can happen if millions of Christians in tens of thousands of churches across the United States would begin doing what the kids at Asbury did: repenting of sin and seeking the Lord earnestly?

What would happen if evangelicals across the US began repenting of their racist attitudes?

What would happen if Christians by the millions started exulting the Lord instead of their country?

What would happen if Christians in droves began making America more 'moral' through exemplifying righteousness that comes through the power of the Holy Spirit rather than depending on flawed political leaders to do so through legislation?

May the spark of the Asbury revival catch fire across our land.

Amen!

Notes

Introduction

1. "Trumpism." *Wikipedia.* Wikimedia Foundation, December 13, 2022. Last modified December 13, 2022. Accessed December 14, 2022. https://en.wikipedia.org/wiki/Trumpism.

2. Geoffrey Kabaservice. "Donald Trump Has Been Defeated, but Trumpism Could Be Here to Stay." The Guardian. Guardian News and Media, November 8, 2020. Last modified November 8, 2020. Accessed April 14, 2023. https://www.theguardian.com/commentisfree/2020/nov/08/donald-trump-trumpism-republicans-democrats.

3. Linda Feldmann. "Why Trumpism Is Here to Stay." The Christian Science Monitor. The Christian Science Monitor, November 5, 2020. Last modified November 5, 2020. Accessed April 14, 2023. https://www.csmonitor.com/USA/Politics/2020/1105/Why-Trumpism-is-here-to-stay.

4   Trisha Ahmed. "North Dakota Governor Signs Trans Athlete Bans into Law." AP NEWS. Associated Press, April 12, 2023. Last modified April 12, 2023. Accessed April 14, 2023. https://apnews.com/article/north-dakota-transgender-lgbtq-sports-ban-04c0f81665e763a63760c793fb67948a.

5   Jonathan J. Cooper. "Kari Lake Loses Suit over Her Defeat in Arizona Governor's Race." NBCNews.com. NBCUniversal News Group, December 24, 2022. Last modified December 24, 2022. Accessed April 14, 2023. https://www.nbcnews.com/news/us-news/kari-lake-loses-suit-defeat-arizona-governors-race-rcna63173.

6   Jeremy Peters and Yamiche Alcindor. "The Party of Trump." Brennan Center for Justice. Last modified April 20, 2023. Accessed April 15, 2023. https://www.brennancenter.org/events/party-trump.

Chapter 1: Biggest Con Job/Marketing Coup Ever?

1   Peter Wehner. "Evangelicals Made a Bad Bargain with Trump." The Atlantic. Atlantic Media Company, October 18, 2020. Last modified October 18, 2020. Accessed March 31, 2023. https://www.theatlantic.com/ideas/archive/2020/10/the-evangelical-movements-bad-bargain/616760.

2   Meghan Keneally. "Donald Trump's Evolving Stance on Abortion." ABC News. ABC News Network, March 21, 2016. Last modified March 21, 2016. Accessed August 11,

2022. https://abcnews.go.com/Politics/donald-trumps-evolving-stance-abortion/story?id=38057176.

3   Harry Beckwith. "The Six Elements of Extraordinary Relationships." Essay. In Invisible Promise: A Field Guide to Marketing in an Upside-down World, page 203. Dallas, Texas: BenBella Books, 2022.

4   "2023 Ford Mustang®: Pricing, Photos, Specs & More." Ford Motor Company. Accessed April 20, 2023. https://www.ford.com/cars/mustang.

5   Eszter Brhlik. "How the Marlboro Man Changed Advertising Forever." Medium. Better Marketing, July 8, 2022. Last modified July 8, 2022. Accessed April 21, 2023. https://bettermarketing.pub/how-the-marlboro-man-changed-advertising-forever-522086774cf4.

6   Harry Beckwith. "The Six Elements of Extraordinary Relationships." Essay. In Invisible Promise: A Field Guide to Marketing in an Upside-down World, Page 100-101. Dallas, Texas: BenBella Books, 2022.

7   Ibid (page 28).

8   Ibid (page 4).

9   Kirstin Kobes Du Mez. "Preface." Preface. In "Jesus and John Wayne: How White Evangelicals Corrupted a Faith and Fractured a Nation," xvii. New York, NY, NY: Liveright Publishing Corporation, a division of W.W. Norton & Company, 2021.

10 Robert P. Jones. Essay in "White Too Long: The Legacy of White Supremacy in American Christianity," p. 15. New York, NY: Simon & Schuster Paperbacks, 2021.

11 Harry Beckwith. "Your Name." Essay. In "Invisible Promise: A Field Guide to Marketing in an Upside-down World," 88. Dallas, TX: BenBella Books, 2022.

12 Nazdar Barzani. "Trump's Biggest Campaign Promises: Did He Deliver?" US Elections 2020 News | Al Jazeera. Al Jazeera, October 31, 2020. Last modified October 31, 2020. Accessed April 22, 2023. https://www.aljazeera.com/news/2020/10/31/trumps-five-big-promises-has-he-delivered-2.

13 Harry Beckwith. "Marketing a Service, Not a Product." Essay. In "Invisible Promise: A Field Guide to Marketing in an Upside-down World," 21. Dallas, Texas: BenBella Books, 2022.

14 Linda Qiu and Annie Karni. "Did President Trump Keep His First-Term Promises? Let's Look at 5 of Them." The New York Times. October 31, 2020. Last modified October 31, 2020. Accessed April 22, 2023. https://www.nytimes.com/2020/10/31/us/politics/trump-first-term-promises.html.

15 Mac Vs. PC - Viruses. YouTube. YouTube, 2009. Accessed April 23, 2023. https://www.youtube.com/watch?v=V0feR5grSa4.

16 Jeremy Diamond. "Trump Escalates Attacks on Clinton's Character | CNN Politics." CNN. Cable News Network, August 6, 2016. Last modified August 6, 2016. Accessed April 24, 2023. https://www.cnn.com/2016/08/05/politics/donald-trump-hillary-clinton-unhinged-lock-her-up/index.html.

Chapter 2: The Church Has Lost Its Way

1 Joel A. Bowman Sr. (2021, September 9). "The Trump Card: How White Evangelicals are Being Played." Baptist News Global. Retrieved October 31, 2022, from https://baptistnews.com/article/the-trump-card-how-white-evangelicals-are-being-played.

2 Jeff Brumley (2018, March 19). "Support for Trump Could Spell End of the Evangelical Church. but When?" Baptist News Global. Retrieved October 31, 2022, from https://baptistnews.com/article/support-for-trump-could-spell-end-of-the-evangelical-church-but-when.

3 Ibid.

4 David Roach, (2021, Nov. 1). "A year after the election, Trump's effect on evangelical churches lingers." News & Reporting. Retrieved October 31, 2022, from https://www.christianitytoday.com/news/2021/november/trump-effects-evangelical-churches-witness-survey-election.html.

5   Andy Stanley, "Chapter One: Battle of the Buckers." Essay. In "Not in It to Win It: Why Choosing Sides Sidelines the Church," 15. Grand Rapids, MI: Zondervan Reflective, 2022.

6   Ibid, 35–42.

7   Meghan Keneally, "Donald Trump's Evolving Stance on Abortion." ABC News. ABC News Network, March 21, 2016. Last modified March 21, 2016. Accessed August 11, 2022. https://abcnews.go.com/Politics/donald-trumps-evolving-stance-abortion/story?id=38057176.

8   "Family Separation – a Timeline." Southern Poverty Law Center. Last modified March 23, 2022. Accessed October 31, 2022. https://www.splcenter.org/news/2022/03/23/family-separation-timeline.

9   Dareh Gregorian, "Trump Told Bob Woodward He Knew in February That Covid-19 Was 'Deadly Stuff' but Wanted to 'Play It down'." NBCNews.com. NBCUniversal News Group, September 9, 2020. Last modified September 9, 2020. Accessed October 31, 2022. https://www.nbcnews.com/politics/donald-trump/trump-told-bob-woodward-he-knew-february-covid-19-was-n1239658.

10 Carolyn Crist, "Birx: Most Covid Deaths Could Have Been Avoided." WebMD, March 29, 2021. Last modified March 29, 2021. Accessed October 31, 2022. https://www.webmd.com/lung/news/20210329/birx-most-covid-deaths-could-have-been-avoided.

11 Eliza Relman, "The 26 Women Who Have Accused Trump of Sexual Misconduct." *Business Insider*, 2020. Last modified 2020. Accessed September 31, 2022. https://www.businessinsider.com/women-accused-trump-sexual-misconduct-list-2017-12.

12 Trump's Access Hollywood Tape: the 48-Hour Fallout. YouTube. YouTube, 2019. Accessed October 31, 2022. https://www.youtube.com/watch?v=cNJGbUWPwe4.

13 Jonathan Allen and Jonathan Stempel, "FBI Documents Point to Trump Role in Hush Money for Porn Star Daniels." Reuters. Thomson Reuters, July 18, 2019. Last modified July 18, 2019. Accessed October 31, 2022. https://www.reuters.com/article/us-usa-trump-cohen/fbi-documents-point-to-trump-role-in-hush-money-for-porn-star-daniels-idUSKCN1UD18D.

14 Larry Neumeister, Michael R. Sisak, and Jennifer Peltz. "Jury Finds Trump Liable for Sexual Abuse, Awards Accuser $5M." *AP News*. AP News, May 11, 2023. Last modified May 11, 2023. Accessed August 3, 2023. https://apnews.com/article/trump-rape-carroll-trial-fe68259a4b98bb3947d42af9ec83d7db.

15 Glenn Kessler, Salvador Rizzo and Meg Kelly. "Analysis | President Trump Has Made 15,413 False or Misleading Claims over 1,055 Days." *The Washington Post*. WP Company, January 17, 2020. Last modified January 17, 2020. Accessed October 31, 2022. https://www.washing

tonpost.com/politics/2019/12/16/president-trump-has-made-false-or-misleading-claims-over-days.

16 Gino Spocchia, "Trump Told 30,000 Untruths during Presidency, Say Analysts." *The Independent*. Independent Digital News and Media, January 21, 2021. Last modified January 21, 2021. Accessed October 31, 2022. https://www.independent.co.uk/news/world/americas/us-election-2020/trump-lies-false-presidency-b1790285.html.

17 Steve Reilly, "USA Today Exclusive: Hundreds Allege Donald Trump Doesn't Pay His Bills." *USA Today*. Gannett Satellite Information Network, April 25, 2018. Last modified April 25, 2018. Accessed October 31, 2022. https://www.usatoday.com/story/news/politics/elections/2016/06/09/donald-trump-unpaid-bills-republican-president-laswuits/85297274.

18 "Donald J. Trump Pays Court-Ordered $2 Million for Illegally Using Trump Foundation Funds ." Donald J. Trump Pays Court-Ordered $2 Million For Illegally Using Trump Foundation Funds | New York State Attorney General. Last modified December 10, 2019. Accessed October 31, 2022. https://ag.ny.gov/press-release/2019/donald-j-trump-pays-court-ordered-2-million-illegally-using-trump-foundation.

19 Tom Winter and Dartunorro Clark, "Federal Court Approves $25 Million Trump University Settlement." NBCNews.com. NBCUniversal News Group, February

6, 2018. Last modified February 6, 2018. Accessed October 31, 2022. https://www.nbcnews.com/politics/white-house/federal-court-approves-25-million-trump-university-settlement-n845181.

20 Nick Visser, "Trump Had 300 Classified Documents at Mar-A-Lago, Called Boxes 'Mine': Report." Yahoo! News. Yahoo!, August 22, 2022. Last modified August 22, 2022. Accessed November 1, 2022. https://news.yahoo.com/trump-had-300-classified-documents-013238569.html.

21 Kristin Kobes Du Mez, "Introduction." Essay. In "Jesus and John Wayne: How White Evangelicals Corrupted a Faith and Fractured a Nation," 3. New York, NY: Liveright Publishing Corporation, a division of W.W. Norton & Company, 2021.

22 Trump Mocks Reporter with Disability. YouTube. YouTube, 2015. Accessed November 2, 2022. https://www.youtube.com/watch?v=PX9reO3QnUA.

23 Donald Trump Under Fire After Hinting Gun Owners Could Assassinate Hillary Clinton. YouTube. YouTube, 2016. Accessed November 2, 2022. https://www.youtube.com/watch?v=Fbv5QFJmdBY.

24 Trump Encourages Cops To Rough Up Suspects-They Applaud. YouTube. YouTube, 2017. Accessed November 2, 2022. https://www.youtube.com/watch?v=9nl00N6I5Ak.

25 Remembering John McCain's Defense of Barack Obama during 2008 Campaign. YouTube. YouTube, 2018. Accessed November 2, 2022. https://www.youtube.com/watch?v=M0u3QJrtgEM.

26 Chelsey Cox, "11 Times Trump Has Ripped Jeff Sessions | CNN Politics." CNN. Cable News Network, November 8, 2019. Last modified November 8, 2019. Accessed November 2, 2022. https://www.cnn.com/2019/11/08/politics/jeff-sessions-donald-trump-insults.

27 Chris Moody and Kristen Holmes. "Donald Trump's History of Suggesting Obama Is a Muslim | CNN Politics." CNN. Cable News Network, September 19, 2015. Last modified September 19, 2015. Accessed November 2, 2022. https://www.cnn.com/2015/09/18/politics/trump-obama-muslim-birther.

28 David Remnick. "Trump Impeachment: Ex-Ukraine Ambassador Yovanovitch Retires." BBC News. BBC, February 1, 2020. Last modified February 1, 2020. Accessed November 2, 2022. https://www.bbc.com/news/world-us-canada-51340094.

29 Veronica Stracqualursi. "Trump Again Mocks Teen Climate Activist Greta Thunberg." CNN. Cable News Network, December 13, 2019. Last modified December 13, 2019. Accessed November 2, 2022. https://www.cnn.com/2019/12/12/politics/trump-greta-thunberg-time-person-of-the-year/index.html.

30 Michael Falcone. "Donald Trump's Holy War? Spokesman Defends 'Get Even' Comment At Christian University." ABC News. ABC News Network, n.d. Accessed November 3, 2022. https://abcnews.go.com/blogs/politics/2012/09/donald-trumps-holy-war-spokesman-defends-get-even-comment-at-christian-university.

31 "Online at Liberty." Liberty University. Liberty University, October 27, 2022. Last modified October 27, 2022. Accessed November 3, 2022. https://www.liberty.edu/online-at-liberty/?acode=D85280&subid=liberty+university&tfn=8558148614&kwid=43700007712193927&device=c&devicemodel=&g_location=9016254&cq_plac=&cq_net=g&cq_pos=&cq_med=&cq_plt=gp&ds_rl=1109193&gclid=CjwKCAjwzY2bBhB6EiwAPpUpZi1dAiqXTMHetnpcx3lu7NSDN3Xmam1fkexoiA_baOxqvldLYdfqqxoCeoYQAvD_BwE&gclsrc=aw.ds.

32 https://www.washingtonpost.com/lifestyle/magazine/jerry-falwell-jr-cant-imagine-trump-doing-anything-thats-not-good-for-the-country/2018/12/21/6affc4c4-f19e-11e8-80d0-f7e1948d55f4_story.html.

33 Lindsey Bever. (November 10, 2016). "Franklin Graham: The media didn't understand the 'God-factor' in Trump's win". The Washington Post. Washington, D.C. Retrieved March 17, 2017.

34 Steve Benen, "This Week in God, 5.12.18." MSNBC. NBCUniversal News Group, May 12, 2018. Last modified May 12, 2018. Accessed November 3, 2022. https://www.msnbc.com/rachel-maddow-show/week-god-51218-msna1100651.

35 Benjamin Fearnow. (November 2, 2019). "Evangelist Franklin Graham urges Prayers for Donald Trump by Promoting T-Shirt". Newsweek. Retrieved December 21, 2019.

36 https://www.theatlantic.com/ideas/archive/2019/11/to-trumps-evangelicals-everyone-else-is-a-sinner/602569.

37 https://www.newsweek.com/billy-grahams-son-says-its-unfathomable-christianity-today-would-side-democrats-totally-1478463.

38 https://www.huffpost.com/entry/franklin-graham-republicans-trump-impeachment_n_6001ebb6c5b6ffcab9644320.

39 https://www.washingtonpost.com/lifestyle/magazine/jerry-falwell-jr-cant-imagine-trump-doing-anything-thats-not-good-for-the-country/2018/12/21/6affc4c4-f19e-11e8-80d0-f7e1948d55f4_story.html.

Chapter 3: Is the Bible Racist?

1 Robert P. Jones. "White Too Long: The Legacy of White Supremacy in American Christianity," 101–101. New York, NY: Simon & Schuster Paperbacks, 2021.

2   https://obu.edu/stories/blog/2020/06/what-does-the-bible-say-about-race.php#:~:text=Using%20cultural%20and%20geographical%20%E2%80%9Cboundary,the%20Israelites%2C%20Canaanites%2C%20Amorites%2C.

Chapter 4: Is Trump Racist?

1   Alana Abramson. "How Donald Trump Perpetuated the 'Birther' Movement for Years." ABC News Network, September 16, 2016. Last modified Septem-ber 16, 2016. Accessed November 6, 2022 https://abcnews.go.com/Politics/donald-trump-perpetuated-birther-movement-years/story?id=42138176.

2   Adam Gabbatt. "Golden Escalator Ride: The Surreal Day Trump Kicked off His Bid for President." Guardian News and Media, June 14, 2019. Last modified June 14, 2019. Accessed November 6, 2022. https://www.theguardian.com/us-news/2019/jun/13/donald-trump-presidential-campaign-speech-eyewitness-memories.

3   https://www.vox.com/2016/7/25/12270880/donald-trump-racist-racism-history.

4   Person. "Trump Slams Haitians Attempting to Enter U.S., Says They 'Probably Have Aids'." ABC7 Los Angeles. KABC-TV, October 11, 2021. Last modified October 11, 2021. Accessed January 31, 2022. https://abc7.com/haitian-migrants-donald-trump-former-president-immigration/11108741.

5. Michelle Mark. "Trump Reportedly Said Haitians 'All Have Aids' and Nigerians Live in 'Huts' during Outburst on Immigration." Business Insider, December 23, 2017. Last modified December 23, 2017. Accessed January 31, 2022. https://www.businessinsider.com/trump-reportedly-said-haitians-have-aids-nigerians-live-in-huts-in-immigration-outburst-2017-12.

6. Eli Watkins and Abby Phillip. "Trump Decries Immigrants from 'Shithole Countries' Coming to US | CNN Politics." CNN. Cable News Network, January 12, 2018. Last modified January 12, 2018. Accessed January 31, 2022. https://www.cnn.com/2018/01/11/politics/immigrants-shithole-countries-trump/index.html.

7. Marietta Vazquez. "Calling Covid-19 the 'Wuhan Virus' or 'China Virus' Is Inaccurate and Xenophobic." Yale School of Medicine, March 12, 2020. Last modified March 12, 2020. Accessed January 31, 2022. https://medicine.yale.edu/news-article/calling-covid-19-the-wuhan-virus-or-china-virus-is-inaccurate-and-xenophobic.

8. "Anti-Asian Hate Crimes Increased by Nearly 150% in 2020, Mostly in N.Y. and L.A., New Report Says." NBCNews.com. NBCUniversal News Group, March 9, 2021. Last modified March 9, 2021. Accessed January 31, 2022. https://www.nbcnews.com/news/asian-america/anti-asian-hate-crimes-increased-nearly-150-2020-mostly-n-n1260264.

9   ABC News. ABC News Network, n.d. Accessed January 31, 2022. https://abcnews.go.com/Politics/trump-mocks-harris-president-insult-country/story?id=72901540.

10 Karen A. Benz. "How Does CEO Behavior Affect Business Culture? • Bettermanager." How Does CEO Behavior Affect Business Culture? BetterManager, June 11, 2018. Last modified June 11, 2018. Accessed August 12, 2022. https://www.bettermanager.co/post/ how-ceo-behavior-affects-business-culture.

11 Katie Reilly. "Donald Trump: Racist Threats Increase after Election." *Time,* November 13, 2016. Last modified November 13, 2016. Accessed August 12, 2022. https://time.com/4569129/racist-anti-semitic-incidents-donald-trump.

Chapter 5: The Scourge of Racism in the Church

1   The Popes, the Catholic Church and the Transatlantic Enslavement of Black Africans 1418-1839. Last modified 2017. Accessed November 6, 2022. https://library.oapen.org/bitstream/id/8aa95306-9256-443f-9e89-de5871874288/external_content.pdf.

2   Sydney E. Ahlstrom. "Part VI: Slavery and Expiation." Essay. In *A Religious History of the American People,* 635–635. London, England: Yale University Press, Ltd. , 1972.

3   Sarah Augustine, "Chapter 1: The Doctrine of Discovery and Me" Essay. In *The Land Is Not Empty: Following Jesus in Dismantling the Doctrine of Discovery*, (page 27). Harrisonburg, VA: Herald Press, 2021.

4   Ibid. (p. 87).

5   Robert P. Jones. "Introduction." Essay. In *White Too Long: The Legacy of White Supremacy in American Christianity,* 6. New York, New York: Simon & Schuster, 2021.

6   Ibid., (pp. 82–88).

7   Wongi Park. "The Blessing of Whiteness in the Curse of Ham: Reading Gen 9:18–29 in the Antebellum South." Nashville, Tennessee, USA: College of Theology and Christian Ministry, Belmont University, October 25, 2021.

8   Robert P. Jones. (2021). In *White Too Long: The Legacy of White Supremacy in American Christianity* (pp. 81–81). essay, Simon & Schuster Paperbacks.

9   Frank S. Mead and Samuel S. Hill, & Craig D. Atwood, C. D. (2001). Southern Baptist Convention. In *Handbook of Denominations in the United States* (pp. 64–64). essay, Abingdon Press.

10 Robert P. Jones (2021). Introduction. In *White Too Long: The Legacy of White Supremacuy in American Christianity* (pp. 2–2). essay, Simon & Schuster Paperbacks.

11 Ibid., (pp. 160–161).
12 Ibid., (p. 43).
13 Ibid., (p. 45).
14 Benjamin Quarles. "The Nonslave Negro." Essay. In *The Negro in the Making of America,* p. 99. New York, NY: Macmillan Publishing Company, 1964.
15 "The Origins of the African Methodist Episcopal Church ..." The Origins of the Schomburg Ctr. for Research in Black Culture Rev. Richard Allen African Methodist Episcopal Church. Accessed March 6, 2022. http://nationalhumanitiescenter.org/pds/maai/community/text3/allenmethodism.pdf.
16 Robert P. Jones. Essay. In *White Too Long: The Legacy of White Supremacy in American Christianity,* 43–44. New York, NY: Simon & Schuster Paperbacks, 2021.
17 Frederick Douglass. "Narrative." Essay. In *Narrative of the Life of Frederick Douglass, an American Slave, Written by Himself,* 60. New Haven, Conn.: Yale University Press, 2016.
18 Ibid. (p. 45).
19 "Lost Cause." *Encyclopædia Britannica.* Encyclopædia Britannica, inc., n.d. Accessed March 10, 2022. https://www.britannica.com/topic/Lost-Cause.

20 Robert P. Jones. Essay. In *White Too Long: The Legacy of White Supremacy in American Christianity,* 80–80. New York, NY: Simon & Schuster Paperbacks, 2021.

21 Ibid. (p. 91).

22 Ibid. (p. 93–94).

23 Ibid. (p. 93-94).

24 Ibid. (p. 93).

25 Ibid. (p. 91–92).

26 Peter Smith, "US Churches Reckon with Traumatic Legacy of Native Schools." *AP NEWS.* Associated Press, July 23, 2021. Last modified July 23, 2021. Accessed January 31, 2023. https://apnews.com/article/canada-religion-e25769edc81d8e1e6639c8960be613d7.

27 Augustine, Sarah. "Chapter 5: We Don't Need Help, We Need Relatives." Essay. In *The Land Is Not Empty: Following Jesus in Dismantling the Doctrine of Discovery,* 94–105. Harrisonburg, VA: Herald Press, 2021.

28 Ibid., (p. 64).

Chapter 6: White Supremacy in the Trump Era

1 Robert P. Jones, Essay. In *White Too Long: The Legacy of White Supremacy in American Christianity,* p. 161. New York, NY: Simon & Schuster Paperbacks, 2021.

2 Ibid., (p. 161).

3 Ibid., (p. 164).

4 "Unite the Right Rally." *Wikipedia*. Wikimedia Foundation, December 20, 2022. Last modified December 20, 2022. Accessed December 29, 2022. https://en.wikipedia.org/wiki/Unite_the_Right_rally.

5 Neiwert, David. "When White Nationalists Chant Their Weird Slogans, What Do They Mean?" Southern Poverty Law Center. Southern Poverty Law Center, October 10, 2017. Last modified October 10, 2017. Accessed December 29, 2022. https://www.splcenter.org/hatewatch/2017/10/10/when-white-nationalists-chant-their-weird-slogans-what-do-they-mean.

6 Meghan Keneally, 8 "What to Know about the Violent Charlottesville Protests and Anniversary Rallies." ABC News. ABC News Network, August 8, 2018. Last modified August 8, 2018. Accessed December 30, 2022. https://abcnews.go.com/US/happen-charlottesville-protest-anniversary-weekend/story?id=57107500.

7 Robert P. Jones, Essay. In *White Too Long: The Legacy of White Supremacy in American Christianity*, p. 161. New York, NY: Simon & Schuster Paperbacks, 2021.bid. (p. 167–172).

8 Ibid., (p. 184).

9 Ibid., (p. 185).

Chapter 7: Keys to Developing an Antiracist Culture

1. Martin Luther King and James Melvin Washington. "Part 5: Books - Stride Toward Freedom (1958) p. 479." Essay. In *A Testament of Hope: The Essential Writings of Martin Luther King, JR.* San Francisco, Calif.: Harper and Row, 1986.

2. Julie Tate, Jennifer Jenkins and Steven Rich. "Fatal Force: Police Shootings Database." *The Washington Post.* WP Company, January 22, 2020. Last modified January 22, 2020. Accessed August 15, 2022.

3. "New Videos Show What Happened before George Floyd's Deadly Encounter with Police." NBCNews.com. NBCUniversal News Group, March 31, 2021. Last modified March 31, 2021. Accessed March 22, 2022. https://www.nbcnews.com/news/us-news/new-videos-show-what-happened-george-floyd-s-deadly-encounter-n1262670.

4. "Charleston Church Shooting." History.com. A&E Television Networks, June 8, 2020. Last modified June 8, 2020. Accessed March 25, 2022. https://www.history.com/this-day-in-history/charleston-ame-church-shooting.

5. Person. "Cops Bought Burger King for Dylann Roof Following His Arrest." ABC7 Los Angeles. KABC-TV, June 23, 2015. Last modified June 23, 2015. Accessed March 25, 2022. https://abc7.com/dylann-roof-south-carolina-church-shooting-emanuel-african-methodist-episcopal/801013.

6 "White Privilege Definition & Meaning." *Merriam-Webster*, n.d. Accessed March 25, 2022. https://www.merriam-webster.com/dictionary/white%20privilege.

7 Peggy McIntosh, *White Privilege and Male Privilege: A Personal Account of Coming to See Correspondences through Work in Women's Studies* (1988). Peggy McIntosh, 1988.

8 Miguel A. De La Torre. Essay. In *Faith and Resistance in the Age of Trump*, 15. Maryknoll, New York: Orbis Books, 2017.

9 Brown Douglas, Kelly. "Charlottesville and the Truth About America – Rev. Dr. Kelly Brown Douglas." Base - Black Theology Project. Last modified February 6, 2018. Accessed August 15, 2022. https://btpbase.org/charlottesville-truth-america.

10 John Harrington, Stacker. "The Trial of Kyle Rittenhouse." Chicagotribune.com. Chicago Tribune, November 1, 2021. Last modified November 1, 2021. Accessed March 28, 2022. https://www.chicagotribune.com/news/ct-kyle-rittenhouse-kenosha-trial-photos-20211117-gijuo7tugfbwba6quzzcgfsv3e-photogallery.html.

11 Todd Richmond. "A Look at Key Points in Kyle Rittenhouse's Testimony." AP NEWS. Associated Press, November 11, 2021. Last modified November 11, 2021. Accessed March 27, 2022. https://apnews.com/article/

kyle-rittenhouse-trial-key-points-bc51f3b9dd0fe0c1289f e2161d7c3ab3.

12 Robert Klemko and Greg Jaffe. "A Mentally Ill Man, a Heavily Armed Teenager and the Night Kenosha Burned." *The Washington Post.* WP Company, October 3, 2020. Last modified October 3, 2020. Accessed March 27, 2022. https://www.washingtonpost.com/nation/2020/10/03/kenosha-shooting-victims.

13 Vanessa Romo and Sharon Pruitt-Young. "What We Know about the 3 Men Who Were Shot by Kyle Rittenhouse." NPR. NPR, November 21, 2021. Last modified November 21, 2021. Accessed March 27, 2022. https://www.npr.org/2021/11/20/1057571558/what-we-know-3men-kyle-rittenhouse-victims-Rosenbaum-lumber-grosskreutz.

14 Julie Bosman. "A Timeline of the Kyle Rittenhouse Shootings and His Trial." *The New York Times,* November 1, 2021. Last modified November 1, 2021. Accessed March 27, 2022. https://www.nytimes.com/article/kyle-rittenhouse-shooting-timeline.html.

15 Kenosha Police Officer Explains Why He Didn't Arrest Kyle Rittenhouse When He Tried to Surrender after the Shootings." Yahoo! News. Yahoo!, n.d. Accessed March 28, 2022. https://news.yahoo.com/kenosha-police-officer-explains-why-015623378.html.

16 The Associated Press. "Prosecutors Add Curfew Charge against Rittenhouse." Wisconsin Public Radio. Last

modified December 30, 2020. Accessed March 28, 2022. https://www.wpr.org/prosecutors-add-curfew-charge-against-rittenhouse.

17 David Roach. "A Year after the Election, Trump's Effect on Evangelical Churches Lingers." News & Reporting. *Christianity Today,* November 1, 2021. Last modified November 1, 2021. Accessed February 6, 2022. https://www.christianitytoday.com/news/2021/november/trump-effects-evangelical-churches-witness-survey-election.html.

18 Alberto-Luperon. "'You Cannot Claim Self-Defense against a Danger You Create': Prosecutor Argues Kyle Rittenhouse's 'Provocation' Invalidates Self-Defense Claim." Law & Crime. Law & Crime, November 19, 2021. Last modified November 19, 2021. Accessed March 28, 2022. https://lawandcrime.com/live-trials/live-trials-current/kyle-rittenhouse/you-cannot-claim-self-defense-against-a-danger-you-create-prosecutor-argues-kyle-rittenhouses-provocation-invalidates-self-defense-claim.

19 Staff, Fox News. "Tucker Carlson on Kyle Rittenhouse: It Was 'Clear' His Case Had 'Deep Implications' for the Rest of Us." Fox News. FOX News Network, December 16, 2021. Last modified December 16, 2021. Accessed March 28, 2022. https://www.foxnews.com/media/tucker-carlson-on-kyle-rittenhouse-it-was-clear-his-case-had-deep-implications-for-the-rest-of-us.

20 Teaganne Finn. "Trump Says He Met with Kyle Rittenhouse after Verdict, Calls Him 'a Nice Young Man'." NBCNews.com. NBCUniversal News Group, November 24, 2021. Last modified November 24, 2021. Accessed March 28, 2022. https://www.nbcnews.com/politics/donald-trump/trump-says-he-met-kyle-rittenhouse-after-verdict-calls-him-n1284513.

21 Jorge Fitz-Gibbon. "Kyle Rittenhouse Lawyer Slams GOP Pols for Offering Teen DC Job." New York Post. New York Post, November 22, 2021. Last modified November 22, 2021. Accessed March 28, 2022. https://nypost.com/2021/11/21/kyle-rittenhouse-lawyer-slams-gop-pols-for-dc-job-offerings.

22 Erin Fine. "Rittenhouse Verdict: Self-Defense Laws Serve White Vigilantes." *The Huntington News.* Last modified January 14, 2022. Accessed March 28, 2022. https://huntnewsnu.com/67506/editorial/rittenhouse-verdict-self-defense-laws-serve-white-vigilantes.

23 Cornell William Brooks. "Cornell William Brooks and the Trotter Collaborative in the Media." William Monroe Trotter Collaborative for Social Justice. Last modified February 11, 2022. Accessed March 28, 2022. https://trotter.hks.harvard.edu/media-mentions-archive.

24 Bubba Wallace. "Ha, Let the Boy Be Black and It Would've Been Life...hell He Would've Had His Life Taken before the Bullshit Trial.. Sad." Twitter. Twitter, November 19, 2021. Last modified November 19, 2021.

Accessed March 28, 2022. https://twitter.com/Bubba Wallace/status/1461768285444317188.

25 "Fired Director of U.S. Cyber Agency Chris Krebs Explains Why President Trump's Claims of Election Interference Are False." CBS News. CBS Interactive, n.d. Accessed March 28, 2022. https://www.cbsnews.com/news/election-results-security-chris-krebs-60-minutes-2020-11-29.

26 Michael Balsamo. "Disputing Trump, Barr Says No Widespread Election Fraud." AP NEWS. Associated Press, December 1, 2020. Last modified December 1, 2020. Accessed March 29, 2022. https://apnews.com/article/barr-no-widespread-election-fraud-b1f1488796c9a98c4b1a9061a6c7f49d.

27 Ryan Goodman, Mari Dugas and Nicholas Tonckens. "Incitement Timeline: Year of Trump's Actions Leading to the Attack on the Capitol." Just Security. Last modified June 13, 2021. Accessed March 29, 2022. https://www.justsecurity.org/74138/incitement-timeline-year-of-trumps-actions-leading-to-the-attack-on-the-capitol.

28 "By the Numbers: The Cost and Consequences of the Jan. 6 Riot." *The Christian Science Monitor,* January 6, 2022. Last modified January 6, 2022. Accessed March 29, 2022. https://www.csmonitor.com/USA/Politics/2022/0106/By-the-numbers-The-cost-and-consequences-of-the-Jan.-6-riot.

29 Betsy Woodruff Swan and Rachael Levy. "Violent Online Messages before Capitol Riot Went Unshared by DHS, Emails Show." POLITICO. POLITICO, January 13, 2022. Last modified January 13, 2022. Accessed March 29, 2022. https://www.politico.com/news/2022/01/13/capitol-riot-online-messages-dhs-527027.

30 Chidozie Obasi. "What Happened at the Capitol Shows White Privilege in Plain View." *Harper's BAZAAR,* June 8, 2021. Last modified June 8, 2021. Accessed March 29, 2022. https://www.harpersbazaar.com/uk/culture/a35148638/what-happened-at-capitol-shows-white-privilege.

31 Kelly M. Hoffman, Sophie Trawalter, Jordan R. Axt and M. Norman Oliver. "Racial Bias in Pain Assessment and Treatment Recommendations, and False Beliefs about Biological Differences between Blacks and Whites." Proceedings of the National Academy of Sciences of the United States of America. National Academy of Sciences, April 19, 2016. Last modified April 19, 2016. Accessed August 15, 2022. https://www.ncbi.nlm.nih.gov/pmc/articles/PMC4843483.

32 "In Focus: Reducing Racial Disparities in Health Care by Confronting Racism." Commonwealth Fund. Last modified September 27, 2018. Accessed August 15, 2022. https://www.commonwealthfund.org/publications/2018/sep/focus-reducing-racial-disparities-health-care-confronting-racism.

33 History.com Editors. "Manifest Destiny." History.com. A&E Television Networks, April 5, 2010. Last modified April 5, 2010. Accessed August 15, 2022. https://www.history.com/topics/westward-expansion/manifest-destiny#:~:text=Manifest%20Destiny%2C%20a%20phrase%20coined,the%20entire%20North%20American%20continent.

Chapter 8: So What Exactly is Racism?

1. FindLaw Attorney Writers. "Movie Day at the Supreme Court or 'I Know It When I See It': A History of the Definition of Obscenity." Findlaw. Last modified 2016. Accessed March 29, 2022. https://corporate.findlaw.com/litigation-disputes/movie-day-at-the-supreme-court-or-i-know-it-when-i-see-it-a.html.

2. "Glossary for Understanding the Dismantling Structural Racism/Promoting Racial Equity Analysis." The Aspen Institute: Roundtable on Community Change, n.d.

3. "Prejudice Definition & Meaning." *Merriam-Webster*, 2022. Last modified 2022. Accessed March 29, 2022. https://www.merriam-webster.com/dictionary/prejudice.

4. Joseph R. Barndt. Essay. In *Dismantling Racism: The Continuing Challenge to White America*, 28–28. Minneapolis: Augsburg, 1991.

Chapter 9: Is America Specifically Ordained by God?

1. "Most Powerful Countries 2022." Most Powerful Countries 2022. World Population Review, n.d. Accessed August 30, 2022. https://worldpopulationreview.com/country-rankings/most-powerful-countries.

2. Richard Wood. "The World's 7 Largest Democracies - Where Do America and India Fit in?" HITC. HITC, October 20, 2017. Last modified October 20, 2017. Accessed August 30, 2022. https://www.hitc.com/en-gb/2017/10/22/the-worlds-7-largest-democracies-where-do-america-and-india-fit.

3. Daniel Lovering. "In 200-Year Tradition, Most Christian Missionaries Are American." Reuters. Thomson Reuters, February 20, 2012. Last modified February 20, 2012. Accessed September 15, 2022. https://www.reuters.com/article/us-missionary-massachusetts/in-200-year-tradition-most-christian-missionaries-are-american-idUSTRE81J0ZD20120220.

4. "Manifest Destiny." *Encyclopædia Britannica*. Encyclopædia Britannica, inc., n.d. Accessed August 29, 2022. https://www.britannica.com/event/Manifest-Destiny.

5. John Avlon. "Baptist Leader Speaks out: 'Christian Nationalism Is Not Christianity'." YouTube. YouTube, September 9, 2022. Last modified September 9, 2022. Accessed September 14, 2022. https://www.youtube.com/watch?v=vZukWuT9lcA&t=190s.

6 Kelsey Vlamis. "Trump Says 'Americans Kneel to God, and God Alone' as Support for Christian Nationalism Grows among Republicans." Business Insider. Business Insider, n.d. Accessed September 14, 2022. https://www.businessinsider.com/trump-americans-kneel-to-god-christian-nationalism-grows-in-gop-2022-7.

7 Paul D. Miller. "What Is Christian Nationalism?" ChristianityToday.com. *Christianity Today*, February 3, 2021. Last modified February 3, 2021. Accessed September 14, 2022. https://www.christianitytoday.com/ct/2021/february-web-only/what-is-christian-nationalism.html.

8 Baptist Leader Speaks out: 'Christian Nationalism Is Not Christianity'. YouTube. YouTube, 2022. Accessed November 14, 2022. https://www.youtube.com/watch?v=vZukWuT9lcA.

9 John Avlon. "Baptist Leader Speaks out: 'Christian Nationalism Is Not Christianity'." YouTube. YouTube, September 9, 2022. Last modified September 9, 2022. Accessed September 14, 2022. https://www.youtube.com/watch?v=vZukWuT9lcA&t=190s.

10 Constantine R. Campbell. "Chapter 1: God and Country." Essay. In Jesus v. Evangelicals: A Biblical Critique of a Wayward Movement, 28–29. Grand Rapids, MI: Zondervan Reflective, 2023.

11 Donald M. Scott. The Religious Origins of Manifest Destiny, Divining America, TeacherServe©, National

Humanities Center. Queens College and the Graduate Center of the City University of New York, September 2013. Last modified September 2013. Accessed September 15, 2022.

12 John Harold Redekop. "What Does God Require of Christian Citizens?" Essay. In *Politics Under God*, 101–102. Waterloo, Ont.: Herald Press, 2007.

13 Miguel A., De La Torre. "Basta!" Introduction. In *Faith and Resistance in the Age of Trump*, xxix-xxx. Orbis, 2017.

14 Mary Fairchild. "Quotes of the Founding Fathers on Religion." Learn Religions. Learn Religions, July 7, 2020. Last modified July 7, 2020. Accessed November 14, 2022. https://www.learnreligions.com/christian-quotes-of-the-founding-fathers-700789.

15 "Handout D: United States Constitution, Amendments 1-27." Bill of Rights Institute. Bill of Rights Institute, n.d. Accessed November 14, 2022. https://billofrightsinstitute.org/activities/handout-d-united-states-constitution-amendments-1-27?gclid=CjwKCAiA68ebBhB-EiwALVC-Nq36B7Xorey7gIWluQOWm8YCigAdZ0JmdTMFnUVPYO8j5XqgcKzXhxoC13cQAvD_BwE.

16 "Treaty between the United States and Tripoli - the U.S. Constitution Online." Treaty Between the United States and Tripoli - The U.S. Constitution Online - USConstitution.net. Last modified January 24, 2010. Accessed

September 29, 2022. https://www.usconstitution.net/tripoli.html.

17 Paul D. Miller. "What Is Christian Nationalism?" ChristianityToday.com. *Christianity Today,* February 3, 2021. Last modified February 3, 2021. Accessed September 14, 2022. https://www.christianitytoday.com/ct/2021/february-web-only/what-is-christian-nationalism.html.

18 Miriam Valverde. "Trump-O-Meter:: PolitiFact." Politifact. The Poynter Institute, December 4, 2018. Last modified December 4, 2018. Accessed September 20, 2022. https://www.politifact.com/truth-o-meter/promises/trumpometer/promise/1422/wont-say-happy-holidays.

19 "Modeling the Future of Religion in America." Pew Research Center's Religion & Public Life Project. Pew Research Center, September 13, 2022. Last modified September 13, 2022. Accessed September 20, 2022. https://www.pewresearch.org/religion/2022/09/13/modeling-the-future-of-religion-in-america.

20 William H. Frey. "The US Will Become 'Minority White' in 2045, Census Projects." Brookings. Brookings, March 9, 2022. Last modified March 9, 2022. Accessed September 21, 2022. https://www.brookings.edu/blog/the-avenue/2018/03/14/the-us-will-become-minority-white-in-2045-census-projects.

21 Paul D. Miller. "What Is Christian Nationalism?" ChristianityToday.com. *Christianity Today,* February 3, 2021. Last

modified February 3, 2021. Accessed September 21, 2022. https://www.christianitytoday.com/ct/2021/february-web-only/what-is-christian-nationalism.html.

22 John Pavlovitz. "White Evangelicals, This Is Why People Are through with You." John Pavlovitz. Last modified August 3, 2022. Accessed September 15, 2022. https://johnpavlovitz.com/2018/01/24/white-evangelicals-people/?utm_campaign=coschedule&utm_source=twitter&utm_medium=johnpavlovitz.

23 https://www.wral.com/fact-check-boebert-says-the-church-is-supposed-to-direct-the-government/ 20365965.

24 "U.S. Constitution - First Amendment | Resources - Congress." Constitution Annotated. Congress.gov, n.d. Accessed September 26, 2022. https://constitution.congress.gov/constitution/amendment-1.

25 George L. Alexander. "Separation of Church and State." Friends Journal. Friends Publishing Corporation, July 30, 2012. Last modified July 30, 2012. Accessed September 26, 2022. https://www.friendsjournal.org/separation.

26 In Jamaica and other British commonwealth countries, public prayer and prayer in schools have been a long-held tradition. For the most part, non-Christians have not publicly raised objections to the practice.

27 Paul D. Miller. "What Is Christian Nationalism?" ChristianityToday.com. Christianity Today, February 3, 2021. Last modified February 3, 2021. Accessed September 14, 2022.

https://www.christianitytoday.com/ct/2021/february-web-only/what-is-christian-nationalism.html.

28 Thomas Acreman. "Roman Emperor Constantine's Conversion to Christianity." Classic History. Classichistory.net, January 14, 2020. Last modified January 14, 2020. Accessed September 28, 2022. http://www.classichistory.net/archives/constantine-christianity#:~:text=Constantine%20is%20the%20first%20Roman,with%20this%20one%20dramatic%20event.

29 Mike Magee. "Christian Atrocities: Three Centuries of Pagan Persecution." Church and State. Church and State, August 29, 2022. Last modified August 29, 2022. Accessed September 29, 2022.

30 Jasmine Alnutt. "The Era of Constantine: When Church Met State." Calvary Chapel. Calvary Chapel, April 23, 2022. Last modified April 23, 2022. Accessed September 28, 2022. https://calvarychapel.com/posts/the-era-of-constantine-when-church-met-state.

31 Paul D. Miller. "What Is Christian Nationalism?" ChristianityToday.com. *Christianity Today,* February 3, 2021. Last modified February 3, 2021. Accessed September 14, 2022. https://www.christianitytoday.com/ct/2021/february-web-only/what-is-christian-nationalism.html.

32 John Avlon. "Baptist Leader Speaks out: 'Christian Nationalism Is Not Christianity'." YouTube. YouTube, September 9, 2022. Last modified September 9, 2022.

Accessed September 14, 2022. https://www.youtube.com/watch?v=vZukWuT9lcA&t=190s.

Chapter 10: How Should the Church Involve Itself in Politics?

1   John Harold Redekop . "Biblical Guidelines Concerning Church-State Relations." Essay. *In Politics Under God,* 31. Scottdale, Pennsylvania: Herald Press, 2007.

2   Ibid., (Page 28).

3   Gailey, Phil. "Reagan, at Prayer Breakfast, Calls Politics and Religion Inseparable." *The New York Times,* August 24, 1984. Last modified August 24, 1984. Accessed September 29, 2022. https://www.nytimes.com/1984/08/24/us/reagan-at-prayer-breakfast-calls-politics-and-religion-inseparable.html.

4   Larry Edelman. "The Economy Cost George H.W. Bush a Second Term. Will the Same Happen to Trump? - The Boston Globe." BostonGlobe.com. *The Boston Globe,* December 3, 2018. Last modified December 3, 2018. Accessed September 5, 2022. https://www.bostonglobe.com/news/politics/2018/12/03/the-economy-cost-bush-second-term-will-same-happen-trump/FXE0ILm4l F3qKw1pXhwshK/ story.html.

5   Kenneth D. Wald and Allison Calhoun-Brown. "Chapter 8: Religion and Conservative Political Mobilization."

Essay. In *Religion and Politics in the United States*, 223. Lanham, Maryland: Rowman & Littlefield, 2018.

6   Andy Stanley. "Chapter 1: Battle of the Buckets." Essay. In *Not in It to Win It: Why Choosing Sides Sidelines the Church*, 17. Grand Rapids, MI, Michigan: Zondervan Reflective, 2022.

7   Constantine R. Campbell. "Chapter 1: God and Country." Essay. In *Jesus v. Evangelicals: A Biblical Critique of a Wayward Movement*, 24. Grand Rapids, MI: Zondervan Reflective, 2023.

8   Ibid., (Page 16).

9   Ibid., (Page 17).

10 Ibid., (Page 13).

11 Ibid., (Page 17).

12 Ibid., (Page 14).

13 Ibid., (Page xx).

14 Allison Calhoun-Brown and Kenneth D. Wald. "Chapter 2: Religion in the American Context." Essay. In *Religion and Politics in the United States*, 31. Rowman & Littlefield, 2014.

15 It's worth noting that members of some Christian groups, including the Amish and some Mennonites, deliberately refrain from political involvement in order to insulate themselves from 'contamination' with the world.

16 Christian A. Eberhart. "Commentary on 1 Timothy 2:1-7." Working Preacher from Luther Seminary. Last modified November 11, 2020. Accessed October 5, 2022. https://www.workingpreacher.org/commentaries/revised-common-lectionary/ordinary-25-3/commentary-on-1-timothy-21-7-3.

17 Steven Pinker. "Chapter 4: The Humanitarian Revolution." Essay. In *The Better Angels of Our Nature: Why Violence Has Declined,* 183. New York, New York: Penguin, 2012.

18 John Harold Redekop. "Chapter 9: Can Morality Be Legislated? Should Christians Practice Pressure Politics?" Essay. In *Politics Under God,* 153. Waterloo, Ont.: Herald Press, 2007.

19 R. N. Murray. "Chapter 10: Anti-Slavery Struggles." Essay. In *Nelson's West Indian History,* 81–90. London: Nelson, 1971.

20 Ibid. Page 83. London: Nelson, 1971.

21 Natasha L. Henry. "Slavery Abolition Act." *Encyclopædia Britannica.* Encyclopædia Britannica, inc., October 4, 2022. Last modified October 4, 2022. Accessed October 13, 2022. https://www.britannica.com/topic/Slavery-Abolition-Act.

22 Juan Williams. *Eyes on the Prize: America's Civil Rights Years, 1954-1965;* with the Eyes on the Prize Production

Team; Introduction by Julian Bond. New York, New York: Viking, 1987.

23 By 1966, the Student Nonviolent Coordinating Committee (SNCC), which grew out of student-led sit-ins at segregated lunch counters, moved beyond the 'nonviolence at all cost' position.

24 Ibid. (Page 79).

25 Ibid. (Page 190).

26 Ibid. "Chapter Six: Freedom in the Air." Essay.

27 Larry Buchanan, Bui Quoctrung and Jugal K. Patel. "Black Lives Matter May Be the Largest Movement in U.S. History." *The New York Times,* July 3, 2020. Last modified July 3, 2020. Accessed October 19, 2022. https://www.nytimes.com/interactive/2020/07/03/us/george-floyd-protests-crowd-size.html.

28 John Harold Redekop. "Chapter Six: What Does God Require of Christian Citizens." Essay. In *Politics Under God,* 107. Waterloo, Ont.: Herald Press, 2007.

29 David Guzik. "Enduring Word Bible Commentary Daniel Chapter 1." *Enduring Word.* Last modified August 23, 2022. Accessed October 27, 2022. https://enduringword.com/bible-commentary/daniel-1.

30 Ben Railton. "Perspective | the Real Message behind That Golden Trump Statue." *The Washington Post.*

WP Company, March 4, 2021. Last modified March 4, 2021. Accessed October 27, 2022. https://www.washingtonpost.com/outlook/2021/03/05/real-message-behind-that-golden-trump-statue.

31 Jenna Johnson. "Donald Trump's Supporters Swear Their Allegiance in Orlando." *The Washington Post.* WP Company, November 26, 2021. Last modified November 26, 2021. Accessed October 27, 2022. https://www.washingtonpost.com/news/post-politics/wp/2016/03/05/donald-trumps-supporters-swear-their-allegiance-in-orlando.

32 "RESOLUTION REGARDING THE REPUBLICAN PARTY PLATFORM," https://www.presidency.ucsb.edu/documents/resolution-regarding-the-republican-party-platform.

33 David Guzik. "Enduring Word Bible Commentary Daniel Chapter 6." *Enduring Word.* Last modified August 23, 2022. Accessed October 27, 2022. https://enduringword.com/bible-commentary/daniel-6.

Chapter 11: The Church's Job: Agents of Reconciliation

1 Constantine R. Campbell. "Chapter 1: God and Country." Essay. In *Jesus v. Evangelicals: A Biblical Critique of a Wayward Movement,* 16. Grand Rapids, MI: Zondervan Reflective, 2023.

2   Henry Clarence Thiessen. "Chapter XXXV - Introductory: Definition and Foundation of the Church." Essay. In *Introductory Lectures in Systematic Theology*, 407. Grand Rapids, Michigan: Eerdmans, 1949.

3   Andy Stanley. "Chapter One: Battle of the Buckers." Essay. In *Not in It to Win It: Why Choosing Sides Sidelines the Church*, 15. Grand Rapids, MI: Zondervan Reflective, 2022.

4   Ed Trevors. Evangelicals: Trump "Used Us." YouTube. YouTube, 2022. Accessed January 8, 2023. https://www.youtube.com/watch?v=xqQ10_7hQ3Y.

5   Ibid.

6   Lior Zaltzman. "A 'Jewish Space Laser' Sounds Funny. but Marjorie Taylor Greene's Anti-Semitism Is No Laughing Matter." St. Louis Jewish Light. Last modified April 21, 2021. Accessed January 10, 2023. https://stljewishlight.org/news/world-news/a-jewish-space-laser-sounds-funny-but-marjorie-taylor-greenes-anti-semitism-is-no-laughing-matter-2/?gclid=CjwKCAiAk—dBhABEiw AchIwkbJVTBACzMevgufEucVrylZFh_CnbuhIiFTj N953wbt7hLb7gDdT1xoCwdEQAvD_BwE.

7   Jasmine Alnutt. "The Era of Constantine: When Church Met State." Calvary Chapel. Last modified April 23, 2022. Accessed October 29, 2022. https://calvarychapel.com/posts/the-era-of-constantine-when-church-met-state.

8   Ibid., xviii.

9   John Harold Redekop. "Chapter 1: Biblical Guidelines Concerning Church-State Relations." Essay. In *Politics Under God,* 35. Waterloo, Ont.: Herald Press, 2007.

10 Andy Stanley. "Chapter 2: Culture War Christianity." Essay. In *Not in It to Win It: Why Choosing Sides Sidelines the Church,* 26. Grand Rapids, MI: Zondervan Reflective, 2022. (Page 26).

Chapter 12: The Church's Goal: Reflect Heavenly Values

1   "Enduring Word Bible Commentary Philippians Chapter 3." *Enduring Word.* Enduring Word, March 16, 2023. Last modified March 16, 2023. Accessed July 27, 2023. https://enduringword.com/bible-commentary/philippians-3.

2   Ibid.

3   Ibid.

4   Cassel, E. T. *I Am a Stranger Here, within a Foreign Land.* The Orthodox Presbyterian Church, n.d. Accessed July 27, 2023. https://opc.org/books/TH/old/Blue695.html.

5   Constantine R. Campbell. "Chapter 2: Exclusion Zones." Essay. In *Jesus v. Evangelicals: A Biblical Critique of a Wayward Movement,* 43. Grand Rapids, MI: Zondervan Reflective, 2023.

6   Ibid., (Page 53).
7   Ibid., (Pages 34-35).
8   Ibid., (Page 35).
9   "The Asbury Outpouring." *Asbury University.* Asbury University, 2023. Last modified 2023. Accessed July 30, 2023. https://www.asbury.edu/outpouring.
10 Ibid.
11 "2023 Asbury Revival." *Wikipedia.* Wikimedia Foundation, July 22, 2023. Last modified July 22, 2023. Accessed July 30, 2023. https://en.wikipedia.org/wiki/ 2023_Asbury_revival.
12 Winter, Tom. "Federal Court Approves $25 Million Trump University Settlement." *NBCNews.Com.* NBCUniversal News Group, February 6, 2018. Last modified February 6, 2018. Accessed October 31, 2022. https://www.nbcnews.com/politics/white-house/federal-court-approves-25-million-trump-university-settlement-n845181.2.

Acknowledgements

I would like to recognize several people—past and present—who helped bring about the writing and publishing of this book. Throughout the process of organizing my thoughts, researching and writing, I recalled the advice given to me by a writing colleague I worked with years ago: Janet Kreider. She was the editor of a publication for which I served as associate editor. On occasions when I passionately pitched an idea for an editorial, Janet would respond, "Go for it. Write it out of your system." Fast forward a few decades, and I'm still following Janet's counsel. Thanks, Janet.

Also, a big thank you to my friend, Robert Charles, for his honest evaluation after reading the first draft of the book. I respect Robert's expertise in the areas of history, political science and theology.

My sister-in-law Reverend Barbara McFarlane also deserves a big thanks for her evaluation of the manuscript. Barbara also recommended a citation program that made endnoting painless.

Bible and religion professor Keith Graber Miller pointed me to the latest texts in the fields of Christian nationalism and political science. Thanks, Keith.

A big shout-out to my friend and former ad agency colleague David Johnson for his excellent cover design. David tweaked the title I gave him and created a concept that artistically captures the tension between Trumpism and citizens of heaven.

Thanks also to the folks at Lucid Books for their partnership in the publishing process. Indeed, members of the team were emphatic that this book *must* get published.

Finally, I wish to thank my dear wife, Annette, for her counsel and moral support through the arduous task of writing the book. Annette was particularly helpful in softening my tone at key points in the manuscript. Thanks, Annette.

www.ingramcontent.com/pod-product-compliance
Lightning Source LLC
Chambersburg PA
CBHW060129190426
43200CB00038B/1898